DREAMS, LIFE, AND LITERATURE

A STUDY OF FRANZ KAFKA

**THE UNIVERSITY OF
NORTH CAROLINA PRESS**
Chapel Hill, 1970

DREAMS, LIFE, AND LITERATURE

A STUDY OF FRANZ KAFKA

CALVIN S. HALL
RICHARD E. LIND

Quotations from the writings of Franz Kafka are
reprinted by permission of Schocken Books Inc., from
The Diaries of Franz Kafka, 1910–1913 © 1948
by Schocken Books Inc.
The Penal Colony by Franz Kafka © 1948
by Schocken Books Inc.
The Diaries of Franz Kafka, 1914–1923 © 1949
by Schocken Books Inc.
Letters to Milena by Franz Kafka © 1953
by Schocken Books Inc.
Letter to His Father by Franz Kafka © 1954, 1966
by Schocken Books Inc.
Quotations from *Franz Kafka: A Biography* by Max Brod © 1947
by Schocken Books Inc., used by permission.

ACKNOWLEDGMENTS

A preliminary draft of this book was read by the following persons: Ralph Berger, Bill Domhoff, John Halverson, Richard Jones, Barry McLaughlin, and Siegfried Puknat, all of the University of California at Santa Cruz; Harold McCurdy, Walter and Sally Sedelow, and Robert N. Wilson of The University of North Carolina at Chapel Hill; Norman Holland of the State University of New York at Buffalo; Richard Howe of the University of Wyoming; William U. Snyder of Ohio University; and Carolyn Winget of the University of Cincinnati.

We are very grateful to them for the careful, discriminating, and knowledgeable reading they gave it. Their comments and criticisms enabled us to make many improvements in the manuscript.

CALVIN S. HALL
RICHARD E. LIND

CONTENTS

DREAMS, LIFE, AND LITERATURE

A STUDY OF FRANZ KAFKA

1. AIMS

Our primary aim is to explore the relationship between what a person dreams about during the night and his behavior and personality during waking life. Few studies of this kind have been reported[1] although psychoanalysts have been using dream analysis for many years to get at the origins and dynamics of neurotic symptoms and character traits.[2] We analyzed the dreams of a person who was not undergoing any kind of psychological treatment at the time he had the dreams, nor to our knowledge had he ever been in therapy (see p. 11). Instead of assessing the individual's behavior and character by means of personality tests—which, in any case, would have been impossible since he died in 1924—we made use of biographical and autographical material in order to find out what sort of a person he was. The dreams were not analyzed by Freud's free association technique nor by Jung's amplification method—which also would have been impossible for the reason stated above—but by objective and quantitative methods recently devised by Hall and Van de Castle (1966a). These methods are based upon the same principles that are used in the content analysis of literature and other verbal material.[3] The only published study comparable to the present one was reported by Hall and Domhoff (1968). They analyzed the dreams of Freud and Jung using the Hall–Van de

1. Studies correlating dreams with various personality tests include the following: Sarason (1944), Grotz (1950), Gordon (1953), Bolgar (1954), Mann (1955), Meer (1955), Shulman (1955), Rychlak (1960), Rychlak and Brams (1963), and Foulkes and Rechtschaffen (1964).

2. An example of the way Freud used dreams in the psychoanalytic treatment of patients will be found in his case study, *An Infantile Neurosis* (1918). The use of dreams in analytical psychotherapy is illustrated by Jung's article, "The Practical Use of Dream-Analysis" (1934). A recent book, *The Clinical Use of Dreams* by Walter Bonime (1962), is a valuable survey of the ways in which dreams are employed in psychotherapy.

3. A survey of these methods is presented in *The Analysis of Communication Content* edited by Gerbner *et al.* (1969). See also *The General Inquirer: A Computer Approach to Content Analysis* by Stone *et al.* (1966).

Castle system and compared the results obtained from biographical and autobiographical sources. A high degree of congruity between their dreams and their waking behavior was observed.

That the dreams we are going to analyze and discuss happen to be those of one of the greatest writers of this century only makes the investigation of greater interest. It is fortunate, for our purposes, that Franz Kafka was one of the few prominent persons for whom a collection of dreams is available in published form.[4] For, in his case, not only is a great deal known about his life—thanks largely to his close friend, literary executor, and

4. Other prominent persons for whom collections of dreams are available in published form are William Dean Howells (1895), Julian Green (1939), Jack Kerouac (1961), Howard Nemerov (1965), Robert Lowie (1966), and Eugène Ionesco (1969). Descartes' famous dreams—three of them in number—have been analyzed by Wisdom (1947) and Jager (1968). McCurdy (1968) has called attention to the dreams of the nineteenth-century German dramatist, Hebbel, which he recorded in his Tagebücher. E. R. Dodds (1965) notes that Aristides published some of his dreams in *Sacred Discourses* and suggests that it would be interesting to make a psychological analysis of them. Many single dreams of famous people have been brought together in an anthology by Brian Hill (1968). A series of dreams by a person who is not prominent will be found in Horton (1925). The Institute of Dream Research has in its files a number of long series of dreams recorded by persons in all walks of life over long periods of time. One of these series provided data for an article by Smith and Hall (1964). Catlin (1965) reports that his dreams have been deposited in the Library of the University of Sheffield, England. Finally, it should not be overlooked that those modern masters of the dream, Freud and Jung, included a number of their own dreams in their writings. Hall and Domhoff (1968) made a content analysis of them and showed that there were congruences between their dreams and their respective personalities. The striking differences in some aspects of their dreams help to explain why the two men proved to be incompatible. Bell and Hall are collaborating on a study of nearly 1,500 dreams recorded by a child molester. Information obtained from a content analysis of the dreams are being correlated with known facts about his life and with data obtained from personality tests and therapy sessions. Doubtless the foregoing references are incomplete. It would be helpful if any readers of this book who know of other published or unpublished collections of dreams would call our attention to them.

biographer, Max Brod,[5] and to a young friend of Kafka's later years, Gustav Janouch—but there are also the published diaries of Kafka which he kept during the same time he was recording his dreams. In fact, most of the dreams were entered in his diaries. In addition to the diaries, some of Kafka's letters have been published including the famous letter to his father and the letters to Milena Jesenská. Of value also were some of the vast numbers of books and articles that have been written about Kafka and his writings. We found works by Politzer (1962) and Sokel (1966) to be particularly helpful. From these various sources one can glean not only the objective facts of Kafka's life regarding family, schooling, travel, work, and friendships, but also rich subjective material relating to his feelings about himself, his family, and the world in which he lived.

Another advantage in using Kafka as a specimen case for exploring the relationship between dreams and life is that he was a writer. This fact enabled us to compare his dreams which are usually regarded as products of unconsciously motivated imagination with his literary works which presumably are more consciously motivated and contrived.

Although our primary objective was not to make a character analysis of Kafka, nor to interpret his writings, it was inevitable that this study would contribute something to both of these topics. The reader will judge how significant these contributions are. We would merely point out with respect to the analysis of Kafka's writings: this is an attempt to apply the same quantitative methods of content analysis to literature that we have used for a number of years in analyzing dreams. We do not wish to engage in polemics regarding the application of such methods

5. Max Brod was born in Prague on May 27, 1884 and died in Tel Aviv on December 20, 1968.

to literature. Numbers and computers are anathema to many people, especially when they are applied in the arts and humanities. A qualitative, subjective, impressionistic methodology is preferred by most critics and interpreters. In the case of the Kafka criticism, it is painfully evident how much chaos a subjective methodology has produced.[6] Whether quantitative methods can do any better remains to be seen. The findings reported in this book suggest that they may.[7]

We undertook this study to try to enlarge our understanding of the significance of dreams in relation to waking life. Over the years, dreams have been explained in many ways. They have been regarded as prophecies or omens sent by gods or ancestors. They have been attributed to environmental conditions acting upon the sleeping person or to internal changes within his body. The contents of dreams have been traced to experiences just prior to going to sleep or during the preceding day or the recent past. Their roots have been found in repressed infantile and birth

6. Several writers have observed that for many critics Kafka's writings are treated like Rorschach ink blots. Each critic projects onto them meanings and interpretations that tell more about the critic than they do about Kafka and his writings.

7. Other types of content analysis have been applied to literature, for example, Spurgeon (1935), White (1947), Schorer (1949), McCurdy (1961), and Sedelow and Sedelow (1966, 1969). The use of content analysis in the humanities as well as in other fields is being expedited by high speed computers (Stone et al., 1966; Gerbner et al., 1969). Ellis and Favat in the book by Stone et al., argue that the computer and the critic can be allies. "The computer does not usurp the critic's essential functions but, in fact, enhances them" (p. 637). This strikes us as being a very sensible statement. An interesting comparison of clinical judgments with content analysis is reported by Allport (1965). The material that was judged or analyzed consisted of 301 letters written by an older woman to married friends of her son. Thirty-six persons were asked to characterize the woman in terms of her traits as expressed in the letters. Eight main traits were identified by the judges. The letters were then content analyzed using a dictionary of 3,000 words and high-speed computers. Many of the same traits identified by the judges emerged from the computerized content analysis.

traumas, fetal experiences, and the collective unconscious. In other words, a dream, according to these genetic or causal theories, is the product of antecedent or concomitant conditions.

But one may also regard a dream as a phenomenon in its own right, irrespective of its origin, and seek to understand how dreams mesh with the dreamer's personality and his behavior in waking life. Dreaming is a form of psychological activity which occurs during sleep. Aristotle defined it very simply as thinking during sleep. It differs from waking mental activity by being hallucinatory in character. In a dream, a person sees himself and usually other people and animals engaged in a variety of encounters with each other and with objects in the environment. Succinctly defined, a dream is an hallucinated behavior episode or series of such episodes in which the dreamer is usually both a participant and an observer.[8] They are not only highly personal documents but they are also sociometric charts in which the dreamer's relations with other people and animals are depicted. Whether these nocturnal behavior episodes, these sociometric charts, provide the same, different, or additional information about the dreamer is the question that interests us.

Our general working hypothesis which was developed out of our extensive experience with dreams is that a person's dreams and his waking behavior are congruent rather than compensatory. A person, we believe, does not change his character when he falls asleep. A sinner does not become a saint. He is the same person awake or asleep. If this is true, one may ask, why not just study the person when he is awake and ignore his dreams. The

8. There are exceptions to this definition. Dreams may consist of thoughts and not of images. Some dreams are merely single images as when a sleeping person has a vision of a face or of an object. In rare cases, the dreamer does not see himself as being in the dream. Usually, however, the dreamer is both an observer and a participant, and he experiences a series of events which may be prosaic, dramatic, or bizarre.

answer is that dreams help to identify and illuminate the meaning and motives of waking behavior. Dreams elude many of the defenses and rationalizations that conceal the wishes and fears which motivate our waking thoughts and actions. Since the publication in 1900 of Freud's monumental work on dreams, they have been regarded as providing information about a person's psychic life that is not readily available from other sources. This study of Kafka's dreams in relation to his life and writings attempts then to furnish empirical evidence for the view that there is continuity rather than discontinuity between dreams and waking life, and to show that dreams extend our knowledge of a person's character.

The steps we took to realize our objectives were the following. First, Kafka's dreams were analyzed using the Hall-Van de Castle system of content analysis. From this analysis, a number of features characteristic of Kafka's dreams were identified. We then went to the biographical and autobiographical sources to see if these features also characterized his waking behavior. A content analysis of some aspects of Kafka's three novels was performed, and the results were correlated with his dreams and with his life. From all of these data, an effort was made to put together a consistent and coherent picture of Franz Kafka. We also speculated on some of the factors in Kafka's childhood that made him the kind of person he was. For the reader who is not familiar with Kafka, a short biography is appended. Kafka's thirty-seven dreams with which we worked are reproduced in a second appendix.

Kafka related thirty-one dreams in his diaries and six in letters to Milena Jesenská. Some of the dreams are only a line or two, while others are long and detailed. The total wordage of the thirty-seven dream narratives is about 9,000. The period during which the dreams were reported was from 1910 to 1923. Kafka was twenty-seven years old in 1910 and forty in 1923. The dreams are reproduced in Appendix B. The following information is given with each dream: page reference, date of the dream, Kafka's age then, comments he made on the dream, and events in Kafka's life at the time of the dream.

We do not know why Kafka chose to write down these particular dreams. He rarely commented on them, nor did he attempt to interpret them. In the case of the dreams he included in letters to Milena Jesenská, it is evident that he was using them as a means of communicating his ambivalent feelings about their relationship. There is evidence that he incorporated some of his dreams in a modified form in his writings. Selma Fraiberg (1963), a psychoanalyst, has dealt with this matter at some length.[1] Many critics have noted the dreamlike quality of Kafka's stories. Sokel (1966), for example, observes that Kafka's writing "conforms to or repeats the activity of the dreaming mind. As Freud has shown in his *Interpretation of Dreams*, a work with which Kafka was familiar, dreams speak in the pictorial language

1. Fraiberg's article makes use of Freud's insights regarding the relation of the artist to his unconscious, and gives a convincing analysis of the way in which Kafka transformed some of his dreams into literature. Unfortunately, the article is flawed by errors of fact. For example, Fraiberg has Kafka contracting tuberculosis in 1922 (it was 1917). She also states that the theme of sexual observation occurs repeatedly in his dreams and writings. Actually, there is no dream in which Kafka watches others having sexual relations, and only one (No. 3) in which he is playing sexually with a woman. It is true that in this dream Max is also with a prostitute but Kafka is too busy with his to pay attention to Max. Dreams of the father, Fraiberg says, occur "monotonously, regularly" when in fact the father appeared in four of the thirty-seven dreams.

speech once was. They take the metaphors hidden in speech literally and act them out as visualized events" (p. 4). Greenberg (1968) is the most recent critic to expound the "dream narrative" form used by Kafka.

Although Kafka infrequently commented on particular dreams, he had a great deal to say about dreams in general. In 1914, Kafka recorded in his diary, "My talent for portraying my dreamlike inner life has thrust all other matters into the background" (D2, p. 77)[2] He reported it was almost impossible for him to sleep because he was plagued by dreams, "as if they were being scratched on me, on a stubborn material" (D2, p. 218). This comparison reminds one of the machine in the story, *In the Penal Colony*, which "scratched" the condemned man's crime on his body. On October 2, 1911, Kafka made this entry in his diary:

Sleepless night. The third in a row. I fall asleep soundly, but after an hour I wake up, as though I had laid my head in the wrong hole. I am completely awake, have the feeling that I have not slept at all or only under a thin skin, have before me anew the labor of falling asleep and feel myself rejected by sleep. And for the rest of the night, until about five, thus it remains, so that indeed I sleep but at the same time vivid dreams keep me awake. I sleep alongside myself, so to speak, while I myself must struggle with dreams. About five the last trace of sleep is exhausted, I just dream, which is more exhausting than wakefulness. In short, I spend the whole night in that state in which a healthy person finds himself for a short time before really falling asleep. When I awaken, all the dreams are gathered about me, *but I am careful not to reflect on them* (D1, pp. 73–74, emphasis supplied).

Kafka expressed a desire to write his autobiography "because it would move along as easily as the writing down of dreams" (D1,

2. D2 refers to the second volume of Kafka's *Diaries*. Other abbreviations for references frequently cited will be found in References, p. 125.

p. 181). Kafka also may have been interested in his dreams in relation to Freudian psychology which Brod claims Kafka knew very well (B, p. 20).[3]

Kafka was not, however, friendly toward psychoanalysis and psychology. Of psychoanalysis he wrote, "There is no pleasure in spending any time on psychoanalysis, and I keep as aloof from it as I possibly can . . ." (Fragments, p. 272). He regarded "the therapeutic claims of psychoanalysis as an impotent error" (Fragments, p. 330). Too much psychology "nauseated" him and he declares, "Never again psychology" (Fragments, p. 50). Kafka satirized the student of psychology as one who has good legs and who if he is admitted to psychology "can in a short time and in any zigzag he likes, cover distances such as he cannot cover in any other field. One's eyes overbrim at the sight" (Fragments, p. 148). Psychology, Kafka enigmatically observes, is impatience (Fragments, p. 73), and for him this was the cardinal sin.

In view of these remarks which suggest more than a reading knowledge of psychoanalysis and because Kafka displayed a number of neurotic symptoms,[4] one wonders whether Kafka may not

3. Hoffman (1959) says "That Kafka should have read Freud is quite probable, for their homes were but a short distance from each other, and for a time at least they were neighbors." The last part of this sentence is puzzling. Freud never lived in Prague, although he was born in Czechoslovakia, and Kafka never lived in Vienna although he often visited it and he was in a hospital there undergoing treatment for tuberculosis shortly before he died.

4. With regard to Kafka's psychopathology a great deal has been written. White (1967) avers that Kafka had flights into psychosis, and others have used such psychiatric labels as "schizophrenic" or "schizoid personality." Neither the present writers nor Selma Fraiberg (1963) feel that Kafka was ever psychotic or had flights into psychosis. After a careful examination of the evidence, Glaser (1964) concludes that Kafka was not psychotic nor was he even neurotic. He was, Glaser believes, normal, perhaps even supernormal.

have consulted a psychoanalyst at some time in his life.[5] Prague
was in the same intellectual orbit as Vienna, a city that Kafka
often visited. Although we do not know what other psychologists, in addition to Freud, Kafka may have read, Brod says he
was not acquainted with the writings of Jung (Fragments, p.
443).

Kafka's thirty-seven dreams were subjected to content analysis.
Content analysis, as Osgood (1959) so cogently describes it,
comprises "methods in which the bias of the analyst is at least
minimized, in which the essential operations can be made ex-
plicit and the conclusions thereby more easily replicated, and in
which the findings can be communicated in meaningful numbers" (p. 34). The method of content analysis used in the present
study was devised by Hall and Van de Castle (1966a) for the
specific purpose of analyzing dreams. It consists of decomposing
a dream into a set of elements, classifying the elements using a
standard list of categories, obtaining frequencies of occurrence of
each category, and comparing the obtained frequencies or proportions with those of a normative or comparison group. It is a
quantitative, objective, and reliable methodology which conforms to Osgood's criteria. One should note that content analysis
generates data but it does not interpret them. Extracting meaning from the data is still largely a subjective task that must be
performed by the investigator.

The Hall-Van de Castle system of content analysis has been
employed in a number of dream investigations. It has been used
to compare the dream contents of men and women (Hall, 1964;
Hall and Domhoff, 1963a, 1963b, 1964; Hall and Van de Castle,
1965), children and adults (unpublished data), ethnic and

5. Edel (1968) also speculates about Kafka having been exposed to
psychoanalysis.

nationality groups (unpublished data), and mental patients and well people (Hall, 1966b). The system has also been employed in studies comparing dreams reported in a laboratory situation with those recalled at home (Domhoff and Kamiya, 1964; Hall and Van de Castle, 1966b). The dreams of Freud and Jung have been subjected to content analysis (Hall and Domhoff, 1968) as well as dreams reported by the climbers of the American Mount Everest Expedition (unpublished data). Although differences in dream contents have been found between all these groups, it should be noted that there are many common elements. There appears to be a fairly large universal pattern in what people dream about irrespective of age, gender, ethnic background, and mental condition. We attribute this universality to those conditions of life which are shared by mankind, as, for example, prenatal existence, birth, a long period of immaturity, bodily features and processes, and so forth.

Thirty-seven dreams reported over a period of fourteen years is a fairly small portion of the dreams Kafka must have recalled during this time. Whether they are representative of his dream life obviously cannot be determined. Nor do we claim they are representative. We can say, however, that the analysis of these thirty-seven dreams, using a quantative methodology, revealed some characteristic themes which are congruent with and help us to understand significant aspects of Kafka's life and character. Moreover, it has been found in previous studies that as few as twenty dreams often give us a pretty good idea of some of the basic preoccupations and conflicts of the dreamer (Hall, 1966a).

The categories used in analyzing Kafka's dreams were objects, characters, aggression, friendliness, sex, misfortune, good fortune, success, failure, emotions, activities, orality, and the castration complex. Each of these categories will be briefly described in presenting the results. A more complete description may be found in Hall and Van de Castle (1966a).

In order to ascertain what is common and what is unique with respect to these content variables in Kafka's dreams, the indices were compared with those obtained from a content analysis of 500 dreams reported by 100 young men between the ages of eighteen and twenty-five. These 500 dreams will be referred to as the normative or comparison sample. The data for them will be found in Hall and Van de Castle (1966a). We shall also occasionally compare the contents of Kafka's dreams with those of Freud and Jung (Hall and Domhoff, 1968).

We digress briefly to discuss the problem of norms since it may be asked what our justification is for comparing the results of a content analysis of the dreams of a famous Jewish writer and lawyer recorded while he was living in Prague from 1910 to 1923 when he was twenty-six to forty years of age with dreams reported by eighteen to twenty-five year old male college students living in Cleveland, Ohio, during the years 1947–1950. From studies we have made, the age difference existing between Kafka and the Cleveland college population appears to have little influence on dreams. The contents of dreams do not change significantly between the age of twenty (the average age of the college students) and thirty (Kafka's average age) (Hall and Domhoff, 1963a, 1963b, 1964). Nor do ethnic and nationality differences between Kafka and the Cleveland sample have much influence upon dreams (Cook, 1956; Winget, 1967; unpublished data). Many of the college students were Jewish, and they like Kafka lived in a large city. Moreover, Kafka was university trained and like some of the college students was a bookish intellectual. Kafka and the college students belonged to different but adjacent generations. Kafka was born in 1883, the average college student was born in 1927. Kafka belonged to the generation of World War I, the college students to the generation of World War II. What data we have indicate that the character of dreams does not change appreciably from one generation to another.

One of our critics (R. M. Jones) has suggested that it is not necessary to show in what respects the contents of Kafka's dreams differ from those of a normative sample since what we are primarily interested in is the congruence or lack of it between his dreams and his personality and not how Kafka differed from other young men. It is correct that we are primarily concerned with exploring the question of correspondences between dreams and behavior, but the subject of our study happens to be a specific individual, Franz Kafka, and not men in general, or a class of men, e.g., writers. It is Franz Kafka's personality and behavior as distinguished from a modal personality and modal behavior that is the focus of our investigation.

An example may help to clarify the distinction. Many more males than females appear in Kafka's dreams. We might conclude from this fact that Kafka was more emotionally involved with men than with women, and look for evidence of such involvement in his waking life. Should such evidence be forthcoming, we might then be tempted to draw a number of inferences about Kafka's "peculiar" or even "abnormal" impulses and attachments. But virtually all males dream more about men than women (Hall and Domhoff, 1963a). In this respect, Kafka's dream life is perfectly normal. Had he dreamed more about women than about men, this fact would have alerted us to look for something unusual in Kafka's waking behavior. Of course, the fact that men usually dream about other men more frequently than they do about women still has to be explained but it cannot be done by means of a single case. Therefore, in the present study, we will limit our attention to the distinctive features of Kafka's dreams, and for this reason a comparison group is required.

The present study rests on the assumption that frequency of occurrence of a given category in a series of dreams is a direct index of the intensity of the dreamer's preoccupation with that category. For example, if we find that there are many more references to parts of the body in Kafka's dreams than in the dreams of the normative sample (as is the case), we conclude from this fact that Kafka's concern with the body was unusually intense. What this signifies and how it originated then has to be determined by considering other information from Kafka's dreams and from his life. What quantitative content analysis does, in short, is to provide the investigator with numerical indices of the outstanding features of a person's behavior in his dream life. These indices may be correlated with one another to find patterns of dream behavior or they may be correlated with indices obtained from waking behavior.

CHARACTERS

A character is defined as a human being, animal, supernatural being, fictitious person, or a group who is referred to in the dream report. Characters other than the dreamer are classified by age, sex, and relationship to the dreamer.

A total of 135 characters appeared in Kafka's thirty-seven dreams. There are not 135 *different* characters since the same character may appear in several dreams. This is an average of 3.6 characters per dream, which is larger than the average of 2.4 characters per dream for the normative group. Kafka is more preoccupied with people than the typical person is. These 135 characters were divided into three categories: single human beings, plural human beings (groups), and animals. The proportion in each category for Kafka's dreams and for the normative sample is as follows:

	KAFKA	NORMS
Single humans	.63	.65
Plural humans	.35	.29
Animals	.02	.06

The proportions for Kafka's dreams do not differ significantly from those for the normative sample. The standard formula for testing the significance of the difference between independent proportions was used throughout this study. If the difference could have occurred by chance no more than 5 per cent of the time, it was considered to be a significant difference.

It is interesting that animals appear so infrequently in his dreams in view of Kafka's short stories in which an animal is the central figure, notably in *Metamorphosis, The Burrow, Investigations of a Dog, A Report to an Academy,* and *Josephine the Singer, or the Mouse Folk.* According to the hypothesis that frequency of occurrence of an element reflects a waking life preoccupation of the dreamer, we would conclude that Kafka was not preoccupied with animals in his waking life. Aside from the aforementioned stories, this seems to have been the case. There is no mention of pets or of reactions to animals in his diaries or in Brod's biography. Kafka does refer to "his dog" in a letter written to Max Brod in 1904 (Politzer, 1962, p. 329) so apparently he or his family did keep a pet at this time in Kafka's life. Animals do not come into any of the three novels except in an incidental fashion. Moreover, when the animal stories are examined, it is seen that Kafka uses the characteristics of animals to represent aspects of the human condition, as, for example, alienation and isolation, and not because of his interest in animals per se. Politzer (1962) observes that "Kafka uses images from the animal sphere to illustrate the human one" (p. 91). This same critic also says that "*The Metamorphosis* is unique among Kafka's animal stories in that Gregor is a human in the form of an animal and not an animal who has been humanized" (Politzer, 1962, p. 65). Nor do the animals in the stories appear to symbolize the primitive side of man's nature as they often do in dreams. When Kafka wishes to depict man's bestiality he uses purely human situations as in *In the Penal Colony*.[6]

In the two dreams where animals play a significant role, they are portrayed as having human characteristics. In Dream 4, the donkey is described as having "narrow human feet," and had never "gone on all fours but always held itself erect like a human being and shows its silvery shining breast and its little belly." The shaggy, blond St. Bernard in Dream 10 also stands on its hind legs.[7]

Ninety-five characters in Kafka's dreams could be identified as either individual males and groups of males or individual females and groups of females. Of these 95, 63 were males and 32 were females which yields a ratio of two males to one female. This is identical with the ratio for the normative sample and appears to be a universal phenomenon (Hall and Domhoff, 1963a). The ratio in female dreams is approximately one to one.

The 132 human characters were then separated into those who Kafka knew, or knew of, in waking life—members of his immediate family, relatives, friends and acquaintances, and prominent

6. The animal theme in Kafka's stories—for it does not occur in his novels—and its relation to totemism is fully explored by Seyppel (1956) within the framework of psychoanalytic anthropology. Kafka had read works on totemism.

7. Van de Castle (1968) has made an extensive analysis of animals in dreams. Animals appear more frequently in the dreams of young children and of primitive people than they do in the dreams of civilized adults. Animals in dreams are often associated with themes of aggression and violence.

persons—and those he did not know. The proportions of familiar and unfamiliar characters in Kafka's dreams compared with those for the normative sample is as follows:

	KAFKA	NORMS
Familiar characters	.41	.45
Unfamiliar characters	.59	.55

The differences between Kafka's proportions and those for the comparison group are again not statistically significant.

Aside from the fact that Kafka's dreams are more densely populated with characters than the dreams of American college students, a fact which suggests Kafka's greater interest in people, there is nothing distinctive about the pattern of characters appearing in his dreams. It reflects characteristics that are universal in male dreams. However, a finer analysis of the characters reveals some interesting features of Kafka's dreams. Kafka dreams about prominent persons more frequently than do those in the normative sample. Eleven prominent persons appear in his dreams whereas the number that would be expected is two. The incidence of prominent people in the dreams of Freud and Jung is also higher than the normative sample. It is possible that persons who themselves are prominent dream more often about other prominent people. We should remind the reader that a prominent person is one the dreamer knows of but does not know personally. It would be natural for famous persons to know other famous people, but when prominent friends or acquaintances of the dreamer are mentioned they are scored as "known" rather than as "prominent."

Kafka's father is an important character in four dreams (Nos. 11, 24, 28, and 36) but his mother appears in only one dream (No. 36) and in that dream she plays a subordinate role. We will have more to say about Kafka's mother and father in his dreams and in his life later.

A distinctive feature of the women in Kafka's dreams is that they are sometimes masculinized. In Dream 7, a girl is playing a male role on the stage. In two other dreams (Nos. 8 and 33), a woman is dressed as a man or is wearing masculine clothes. In the light of what we will have to say later about the probable origin of Kafka's conception of women as being masculinized, Dream 8 is of significance. Kafka dreams he is in a theater and people are coming in. ". . . my attention is called especially to a married couple forcing their way along a row of seats, since the woman has a dark-yellow, mannish, long-nosed face and besides, as far as one can see in the crowd out of which her head towers, is wearing men's clothes. . . ." Dream 33 refers to Milena of whom Kafka dreamed, "Your dress, strangely enough, was from the same material as my suit, was also very masculine, and I really didn't like it at all." The identification between Kafka and Milena is also depicted in Dream 37.

We kept merging into one another, I was you, you were me. Finally, you somehow caught fire. I took an old coat and beat you with it. But again the transmutation began and it went so far that you were no longer even there, instead it was I who was on fire and it was also I who beat the fire with the coat. In the meantime, the fire brigade arrived and somehow you were saved. But you were different from before, spectral, as though drawn with chalk against the dark, and you fell, lifeless or perhaps having fainted from joy at having been saved into my arms. But here too the uncertainty of transmutability entered. Perhaps it was I who fell into someone's arms.

Although the sexual symbolism in this dream is transparent, it is the transformation of a man into a woman and a woman into a man that we wish to point out as being of significance. Kafka not only sees women as being masculine but he also sees himself as changing into a woman; an extremely rare happening in male dreams. Kafka avers that he had a pronounced talent for metamorphosing himself (D1, p. 71), and his most famous short story is called *Metamorphosis*. In this story, however, a man is changed into an insect and not into a female. It may also be relevant to the present discussion to note that the hero of *The Trial* is a male human being named Joseph, and the heroine of one of Kafka's last stories is a female mouse named Josephine (*Josephine the Singer, or the Mouse Folk*).

AGGRESSION

An aggression is defined as any form of implicit, verbalized, or physical expression of hostility between two or more characters. There is also a category of self-aggression but this category was not represented in Kafka's dreams. At least one aggression occurred in fifteen of Kafka's thirty-seven dreams. This proportion of .41 is not significantly different from the proportion of .47 for the normative sample. Another method of figuring the incidence of aggression is to divide the total number of aggressions by the total number of characters. There were twenty-four separate acts of aggression in Kafka's dreams. When this figure is divided by the number of characters (135), the resulting proportion is .18. The comparable proportion for the normative sample is .34 which is almost twice as large as Kafka's proportion. The difference between the two proportions is significant at less than the .001 level of confidence.

Not only does Kafka have fewer aggressions in his dreams, but the intensity of the aggression is lower than the norms. The proportion of physical aggression is .38 in Kafka's dreams and .50 in the comparison group. The difference between these two proportions is not statistically significant, however.

The total number of aggressions was separated into those in

which the dreamer was involved and those which he witnessed. There were fifteen of the former and nine of the latter type. When compared with the norms, the proportion of each type is as follows:

	KAFKA	NORMS
Dreamer involved aggression	.62	.80
Witnessed aggression	.38	.20

The difference between Kafka's proportions and the norms is significant at less than the .05 level of confidence. Kafka witnesses more aggressiveness than the norm group does which ties in with the scoptophilic theme to be discussed later. Kafka's pattern of witnessed and personally involved aggressions is almost identical with that of Freud's, whereas Jung's is the same as the normative group.

However, when Kafka does become involved in an aggression, he is more likely to be the aggressor than the victim. This is contrary to the norms as the following table shows.

	KAFKA	NORMS
Dreamer aggressor	.60	.31
Dreamer victim	.20	.48

That Kafka could have sadistic dreams as well as write sadistic stories is illustrated by Dream 25 in which he and a group of men hold a man's foot against a red-hot oven door until it smokes. Kafka remarks, "Unfortunately, we had no knife with which to stab him." The masochistic side of Kafka's nature expresses itself in Dream 30 in which he says, "My feeling of happiness lay in the fact that I welcomed so freely, with such conviction, and with such joy, the punishment that came." These examples should not lead one to conclude that Kafka was unusually sado-masochistic in his dreams. He was actually less so than the typical male dreamer.

Kafka becomes involved in more aggressions with males than with females, but since there are twice as many male characters as female characters, a correction should be made for this difference. This is done by dividing the number of aggressions with males by the number of male characters, and the number of aggressions with females by the number of female characters. The proportions obtained for Kafka's dreams and for the normative sample are as follows:

	KAFKA	NORMS
Aggression with males / No. of male characters	.11	.28
Aggression with females / No. of female characters	.13	.17

The difference between Kafka's proportion of aggressions with males and the proportion for the normative sample is significant at less than the .01 level of confidence. The difference between the proportions of aggressions with females is not a significant one. In other words, Kafka has the expected number of aggressive interactions with females, but significantly fewer with males. We will have more to say about this finding further on.

To summarize, of the seven indices of aggression that were computed for Kafka's dreams, three did not differ significantly from the norms and four did. His dreams contained fewer aggressions relative to the number of characters, more witnessed aggression, more aggression in which he initiated the aggression, and fewer aggressive interactions with males. Probably the outstanding feature of these results is that the relatively low number of aggressions in Kafka's dreams is due to a paucity of aggressive encounters between Kafka and other males.

FRIENDLINESS

A friendly interaction is defined as one in which one character greets another character in a friendly manner, gives or loans something, does a favor or helpful act, or expresses affection.

The incidence of friendly interactions in Kafka's dreams is the same as the incidence of aggressive interactions, 24 versus 24. In the normative sample, aggressions outnumber friendly encounters. When a statistical test was made of the difference between the incidence of friendliness in Kafka's dreams and the norms, it turned out to be insignificant. Likewise, when the number of friendly interactions was divided by the number of characters, the resulting proportion of .18 for Kafka did not differ significantly from the proportion of .21 for the comparison group.

An analysis of dreamer-involved versus witnessed friendliness in Kafka's dreams and in the norm group did not show any difference. Nor did an analysis of the dreamer as befriender versus dreamer as befriended.

Kafka's friendly interactions with male characters relative to the number of male characters is nearly the same as his friendly interactions with female characters relative to the number of female characters. This differs, but not significantly, from the norms as the following table shows.

	KAFKA	NORMS
Dreamer friendly with males / No. of male characters	.16	.17
Dreamer friendly with females / No. of female characters	.19	.29

With regard to friendliness, then, Kafka's dreams are not distinctively different from the norms.

A COMPARISON OF AGGRESSION AND FRIENDLINESS

A comparison of Kafka's aggression and friendliness involving male and female characters with the norms is presented in the following table. The four proportions in each half of the table form what we call an A-F square. In other studies, the A-F square provided important information about mental patients (Hall, 1966b), differences in the personalities of Freud and Jung (Hall and Domhoff, 1968), and differences between males and females (Hall and Van de Castle, 1966a).

	KAFKA	
	Aggressive	Friendly
With males	.11	.16
With females	.13	.19

	MALE NORMS	
	Aggressive	Friendly
With males	.28	.17
With females	.17	.29

It will be noted that the typical pattern in male dreams is a relatively high incidence of aggression with males and a relatively high incidence of friendliness with females. This is what one would expect to find either on the basis of everyday observation or on a theoretical basis, e.g., Freud's theory of the Oedipus complex. The typical male is more likely to see other males as enemies and females as friends.

Kafka's pattern differs from the typical one by showing a similar incidence of aggression and friendliness with both males and females. In other words, Kafka has mixed feelings toward the members of each sex in his dreams. Neither sex stands out as being either an enemy or a friend. Kafka's pattern is more like the typical pattern found in female dreams as the following comparison shows.

	KAFKA	
	Aggressive	*Friendly*
With males	.11	.16
With females	.13	.19

	FEMALE NORMS	
	Aggressive	*Friendly*
With males	.22	.24
With females	.14	.15

Females also have mixed feelings for the same and opposite sex; thus we see similar proportions of aggression and friendliness in their dreams. Unlike males, they are not sure who their friends or enemies really are. Likewise, with Kafka, his proportions are close, thus denoting a similar ambivalent attitude toward males and females. In our study of the dreams of Freud and Jung (Hall and Domhoff, 1968), we found that Freud had more aggressive encounters with females than with males, and more friendly interactions with males than with females. Jung's pattern was similar to that of the normative group. From these results we concluded that Freud had an inverted Oedipus complex and Jung had a typical one for males. Kafka fits into neither of these types. His Oedipus complex is not inverted nor is it normal; rather it is more like the female version of the Oedipus complex.

Much of Kafka's ambivalence toward males in dreams is directed against his father, as it was also in waking life. In Dream 36, he threatens to kill his father (or himself) if he says anything bad about Milena. He characterizes his father's ideas on social reform as old and outworn in Dream 28. In Dream 11, Kafka emulates his father's feat in scaling a wall and his father "fell on my neck and kissed and embraced me." Kafka, however, resented the fact that his father did not help him scale the wall which was covered with human excrement. Probably the most revealing dream concerning his father is Number 24. Kafka holds onto his father who is leaning out the window, and endangers himself thereby. But he cannot let go of his father even to save himself.

Kafka's ambivalent feelings about women are strongly evidenced in the six Milena dreams. In Dreams 33, 34, and 35 he feels rejected by Milena, in Dream 32 he is unable to communicate with her, in Dream 36 he kills a male relative for saying something offensive about Milena, and in Dream 37 he and Milena are consumed by flames as they merge into one another.

SEX

Overt sexual activity occurs in only one of Kafka's dreams. The expected number would be four according to the norms. In his one sex dream (No. 3), Kafka and a friend are engaging in sex play with a pair of whores in a brothel. "I fingered her legs and then for a long time pressed the upper parts of her thighs in regular rhythm. My pleasure in this was so great that I wondered that for this entertainment, which was after all really the most beautiful kind, one still had to pay nothing. I was convinced that I, and I alone, deceived the world." The deception does not last long, however, because Kafka discovers to his horror that the whore's body is covered with red splotches, particles of which rub off on his fingers. This is an instance of the body disfigurement theme which runs through Kafka's dreams, and about which we will have more to say.

One of our critics suggested that the difference in the incidence of sex dreams between Kafka and the normative group may be due to age. In a number of dream series obtained from men the same age as Kafka was when he recorded his dreams, and from older men, sex dreams occur with greater frequency than they do for Kafka. We do not feel that age, at least within the age range from twenty to thirty, influences significantly the incidence of sex dreams. The incidence of nocturnal emissions in single males does not decrease materially between the ages of twenty and thirty according to figures given in Kinsey, Pomeroy, and Martin (1948, p. 243).

SUCCESS AND FAILURE

Success and failure occur about equally often in Kafka's dreams —nine to ten—which corresponds to the norms. Failure to the dreamer constitutes .80 of all failures which is not significantly different from the norm proportion of .86. With regard to success, however, Kafka experiences much less than the norms. The proportions are .56 for Kafka and .89 for the comparison group. The difference is significant at the .01 level of confidence. This means that Kafka achieves success less frequently in his dreams than the average male college student does.

MISFORTUNE AND GOOD FORTUNE

A misfortune is a mishap which happens to the dreamer or to a character over which he has no control. It is not the result of a hostile act. A good fortune is something that happens to the dreamer or another character which is not the result of a friendly act or the consequence of trying to achieve a goal.

The number of dreams in which a misfortune occurs to Kafka or to another character is 19 which yields a proportion of .51. The corresponding proportion for the normative sample is .36. The difference between these two proportions is not significant.

Good fortune is rare in dreams occurring in six out of every one hundred dreams of the normative sample. Kafka has four dreams in which a good fortune occurs, which again is not significantly different from the norms.[8]

8. In every group whose dreams we have analyzed, some fifty in all

EMOTIONS

An analysis of the types of emotions experienced by Kafka in his dreams does not reveal any significant differences from the norms, as the following table shows.

	KAFKA	NORMS
Happy	.31	.21
Sad	.12	.09
Angry	.04	.12
Confusion	.12	.23
Fear and guilt	.42	.35

The fear and guilt category consists primarily of dreams in which Kafka feels afraid or apprehensive. Guilt is implied in only one dream (No. 30), and even in reporting this dream Kafka does not say explicitly that he felt guilty. In this dream, Kafka's brother commits a crime in which Kafka is implicated, and he (Kafka) welcomes the punishment that follows. This "welcome punishment" may be interpreted as a sign of a guilty conscience. In another dream (No. 3), Kafka felt abashed to be walking through a room in which people were lying in bed, but this feeling is not so much guilt as embarrassment.

In view of the theme of guilt which so many critics have found in Kafka's writings, *The Trial* being the most notable example, and Kafka's own admission that he had a boundless sense of guilt, it is surprising that there is a dearth of guilt in his dreams. He may, of course, have failed to report such dreams but this is not likely if he were really preoccupied with guilt in his waking life. Nor is an explanation in terms of repression very convincing

---

differing in age, sex, and ethnic and national background, misfortunes exceed good fortunes by a large amount. Apparently, it is universal for people to see themselves in their dreams as the victims of circumstances over which they have no control.

since one does not repress in his dreams what he so readily expresses in waking life. It is possible that guilt was disguised in his dreams but, if so, a careful scrutiny of them failed to penetrate the disguise. Perhaps a more acute analyst can find in Kafka's dreams the guilt that we have been unable to locate. The question of guilt in Kafka's life and in his writings will be discussed in a later chapter.

ACTIVITIES

No class of activity engaged in by Kafka in his dreams differs significantly from the norms. The proportions are as follows:

	KAFKA	NORMS
Verbal	.26	.22
Physical	.29	.26
Movement	.16	.22
Location change	.04	.08
Visual	.18	.14
Hearing	.02	.02
Expressive	.00	.01
Cognitive	.05	.04

There is one striking difference, however, with respect to activities. The proportion of activities in which Kafka engages relative to the total number of activities engaged in by all characters is less than the norm proportion, as the following table shows.

	KAFKA	NORMS
Dreamer's activities / Total activities	.52	.76
Activities of others / Total activities	.48	.24

The difference is significant at less than the .001 level of confidence.

OBJECTS

In the Hall-Van de Castle method of content analysis, objects appearing in dream narratives are classified under thirteen headings. The distribution of the 377 objects mentioned in Kafka's dreams, and the norm proportions are presented in the following table.

	KAFKA Frequency	p	NORMS p
Architecture, e.g., buildings, rooms, etc.	79	.210	.271
Household, e.g., table, dishes, etc.	32	.085	.082
Food	6	.016	.018
Implements, e.g., tools, guns, recreational equipment	12	.032	.066
Travel, e.g., auto, train	24	.064	.112
Streets	20	.053	.067
Nature	23	.061	.091
Regions	19	.050	.056
Body parts	111	.295	.102
Clothing	32	.085	.057
Communication, e.g., books, typewriter, pencil, paper	14	.037	.039
Money	0	.000	.015
Miscellaneous	5	.013	.025

The outstanding feature of this table is the close correspondence between Kafka's proportions and those of the norms with one glaring exception, that of body parts. This category consists of any reference to the body—hair, eyes, face, beard, legs, toes, internal organs, and excretions. There are nearly three times more references to the body in Kafka's dreams than in the norm dreams. The difference is significant at less than the .001 level. This suggests that Kafka was preoccupied with the body in his dreams, as we shall see he was also in waking life.

An examination of the dreams in which the body is referred to shows that in seven of them the theme of disfigurement occurs. A whore with whom Kafka is having sex play has a skin disease (Dream 3). In Dream 8, a young woman has a "scratched bloodshot spot the size of a doorknob" on her right hip. In two dreams, Nos. 35 and 1, the face of a woman is disfigured and in two other dreams (Nos. 2 and 16), the disfigurement of a character takes the form of blindness. Kafka dreams about his own disfigurement in Dream 31.

Two other differences may be noted. There are more references to clothing in Kafka's dreams (significant at the .05 level). In Dream 5, for example, he describes in great detail the clothes of an Englishman he meets. Even his face was covered with a gray material, "new, napped, rather like flannel, very flexible and soft, of excellent English manufacture. All this pleased me so, that I was eager to become acquainted with the man." This emphasis on clothing, which we shall see is also a waking preoccupation with Kafka, has a countermanifestation, that of the naked body. There are five dreams in which a naked person or persons appear. In five dreams, hair or beard, which are coverings for the naked body, are described. What these themes of clothes, nakedness, and hair mean will be discussed later.

Nature is referred to less often in Kafka's dreams than in the dreams of the comparison group although the difference is not very great. We mention it because at least two writers on Kafka have noted the absence of nature imagery in his writings. Urzidil (1968) who knew Kafka in Prague observes "As a man Kafka was surely a friend of nature. However, in his writings and diaries viable nature is rarely mentioned . . ." (p. 57). Urzidil performed a content analysis of the 700 pages of Kafka's diaries covering a period of fourteen years and found that references to nature or to landscape occur scarcely ten times and then only incidentally. Erik Heller (1969) says that apart from mention of a starry sky, wind, and snow, "there is not one mention of nature in *The Castle*" (p. 44).

We did a spot check of references to clothes and to body parts in the *Diaries*, and found that clothes were mentioned on every other page, and body parts on eight out of every ten pages. Often there were as many as five to ten mentions of parts of the body on a single page.

ORAL INCORPORATION

Oral incorporation is defined as eating or drinking, mention of food, being in a restaurant, cooking, etc. The term "oral incorporation" has been taken from Freudian theory. The proportion of dreams in the normative sample that contain some oral incorporation is .16. Kafka's proportion is .18 which is not significantly different from the norms, and again shows the close correspondence between Kafka's dreams and those of the comparison group.

CASTRATION COMPLEX

The castration complex as described by Freud consists of three aspects: castration anxiety, castration wish, and penis envy. Castration anxiety is defined as an injury to a part of the dreamer's body or harm to one of his possessions. Castration wish is defined as harm to another character's body or to one of his possessions. Penis envy is defined as the acquisition of a phallic object by the dreamer, e.g., automobile, gun, sword. These are theoretical categories derived from Freudian psychology and along with oral incorporation are unlike the other categories used in this study which are empirical in nature.

There are no instances of castration anxiety in any of Kafka's dreams although according to the norms one would expect to find seven or eight such dreams. A boil on Kafka's cheek in Dream 31 is not scored as castration anxiety since it is a blemish and not a loss, injury, or defect of a part of the body (Hall and Van de Castle, 1966a, pp. 126–30). There are two dreams that contain a castration wish, and one which contains penis envy. The dream (No. 22) in which penis envy occurs is particularly striking. Friends discover a large sword "buried to the hilt" in Kafka's back. They withdraw the sword which has been placed "with such incredible precision between my skin and flesh that it had caused no injury," and hand it to Kafka. "I hefted it in my two hands; it was a splendid weapon...." The incidence of castration wish and penis envy do not differ from the norms. What does differ, however, is that the incidence of castration wish *plus* penis envy is greater than the incidence of castration anxiety. This is typical of *female* dreams but not of male dreams (Hall and Van de Castle, 1965).

SCOPTOPHILIA

It has already been noted that Kafka witnesses rather than participates in aggression to a greater extent than the normative group does. He also watches other people carry on activities more often than the typical male dreamer does. In eleven of the thirty-seven dreams Kafka is a spectator throughout the dream rather than a participant. This is a much higher incidence than is ordinarily found.

This "voyeuristic" motif is vividly expressed in two dreams in which Kafka is at the theater. He describes in detail what takes place on the stage and in the audience. In one of these theater

dreams (No. 8) a reaction formation against "looking" is represented by his sitting in a seat that faces away from the stage, and
by not being able to see the stage clearly because people block his
view. In another dream (No. 3), the reaction formation is expressed by his not turning his head to look at people who are in
bed. In Dream 9, he is looking at a picture by Ingres in which
there is a naked girl "but there was too much nakedness left in
this girl even for the sense of touch." Glass walls appear in three
dreams which is most unusual, and blindness which may be considered a reaction formation against the desire to look is found
in two dreams.

This completes the quantitative content analysis of Kafka's
dreams. In many respects what Kafka dreams about does not
differ from what the average young male dreams about. This
finding agrees with other studies that have been made of individual dreamers. There is a great deal of universality in the contents of dreams. This universality is due, we believe, to a common
ontogeny and set of experiences shared by all human beings.
These developmental commonalities, which consist of such
things as a prenatal period, birth, a long period of immaturity,
maturational sequences, eating, and elimination, provide the
basis for a common set of human problems, frustrations, and
conflicts that then express themselves in dreams as well as in
waking life.

In addition to these common elements, dreams also contain
material that is specific to the individual dreamer. It is not so
much that dreamers have different problems as that a particular
problem manifests itself in a stronger or weaker form in the
dreams of different people. Freud has formulated the general
hypothesis in this manner: ". . . we are tempted to say that the
elements of the psychic constitution are always the same. What
changes in the mixture is the quantitative proportion of the ele-

ments and, we must add, their location in different fields of the psychic life and their attachment to different objects" (Freud, 1967). For example, probably everyone is preoccupied to some extent with his body but in Kafka's dreams this preoccupation is particularly strong. Since we are interested in showing that the singular features of Kafka's dreams are related to characteristics of his waking behavior and personality, our attention will be focused on the unusual themes that have been identified in Kafka's dreams.

SUMMARY

Seven themes stand out in Kafka's dreams. These themes and the empirical data from which they have been derived are as follows:

Preoccupation with the Body—This concern is evidenced by the very high incidence of references to body parts in Kafka's dreams.

Body Disfigurement—Disfigured bodies occur fairly frequently in Kafka's dreams.

Emphasis on Clothing and Nakedness—References to clothing and to nakedness exceed those of the comparison group.

Scoptophilia—This theme is represented by looking and witnessing, by reaction formations against looking, by glass walls, and by blindness.

Passivity—Kafka's passivity in his dreams is indicated by a low incidence of aggression, of sex, of personal success, and of activities in which Kafka engages.

Ambivalence toward Men and toward Women—Kafka displays a virtual equality in the relative incidence of aggression and friendliness with males and with females. This is an atypical pattern for male dreamers.

The Masculinized Woman—In some dreams, Kafka describes

a female character as being masculine in appearance or dress. This rarely occurs in male dreams.

In the next chapter, we will present evidence from Kafka's diaries and letters, and from biographical material, to show that these seven themes preoccupied Kafka during his waking life as well.

3. DREAMS AND WAKING BEHAVIOR

Following the analysis of Kafka's dreams we consulted the main sources of information about Kafka's life and character. These are his diaries which he kept between 1910 and 1923, the letters he wrote to Milena Jesenská from 1920 to 1923, the letter to his father written in 1919, Max Brod's biography, letters to other friends from 1900 to 1924 (Kafka, 1958), the eight octavo notebooks and fragments from notebooks (Kafka, 1954), and Janouch's *Conversations with Kafka* (1953). Some secondary sources were also consulted but since these depend upon the foregoing books for their information about Kafka, they added little to our knowledge of him.[1]

Politzer (1962, p. 18) cautions the reader to treat Kafka's diaries, letters, and conversations with extreme circumspection because he feels the information they contain is often misleading. In order to avoid drawing conclusions from faulty data we made an effort to obtain evidence for the presence of those traits in which we were interested both from Kafka's diaries and letters and from independent observers, principally Max Brod. Brod, because of his proprietary interest in Kafka, may not always be a purely objective observer. With respect to many of the traits,

1. The criticism may be made that having first analyzed the dreams we then proceeded to select only that information from the life history material which would support the characteristics found in Kafka's dreams and ignored any contradictory evidence. Obviously, we did look for material in the diaries, letters, and biographies that bore some relation to the seven themes identified by the content analysis of the dreams. But aware of the possibility of biased selection we exercised care in examining the primary sources. We were not content to rest our case upon one or two bits of evidence which might be atypical or insignificant. The evidence from the primary sources regarding the themes in Kafka's dreams was so overwhelming in some cases and so clearly presumptive in others we are confident that anyone who went over the same material would observe them too. The way in which the information obtained from objective and subjective sources, from the dreams, and from the novels hangs together with so much internal consistency is probably the most convincing evidence for the validity and reliability of the findings and interpretations.

however, there is no reason why either Kafka himself or Brod should have been misleading since they do not reflect adversely upon Kafka's character. Furthermore, we had to be convinced by the weight of evidence from all of the sources that the trait in question was a prominent one in Kafka's behavior. The same criterion of frequency used in identifying the predominant and characteristic features of Kafka's dream life was employed to identify Kafka's characteristic behavior during waking life. We hope this will become evident to the reader in the following discussion.

Politzer (1962) also questions the value of Kafka's letter to his father for understanding the "real" Kafka. He calls it a parable and says its documentary value is minimal (p. 293). Granted that it contains special pleading—Kafka told his friend, Milena, that it was a "lawyer's letter" (M, p. 79)—there are still a number of objective descriptions of events in it which we believe are valid as documentary material.

The emphasis in this chapter as in the preceding one falls on the empirical rather than on the inferential or interpretive. Inferences about Kafka's personality drawn from the empirical findings will be postponed until a later chapter.

PREOCCUPATION WITH THE BODY

We inferred from the large number of body references in Kafka's dreams that he was preoccupied with his own body. Numerous entries in his diaries make it painfully evident that this indeed was the case in his waking life. In 1910, seven years before tuberculosis was diagnosed, he wrote of the "despair over my body and over a future with this body" (D1, p. 11). A little later, however, he noted that "my calves are good, my thighs are not bad, my belly will pass muster, but my chest is very shabby" (p. 14). He considered himself to be weak and skinny. "My body is too long for its weakness, it hasn't the least bit of fat to engender a blessed warmth, to preserve an inner fire, no fat on which the spirit could occasionally nourish itself beyond its daily need without damage to the whole. How shall the weak heart that lately has troubled me so often be able to pound the blood through all the length of these legs. It would be labor enough to the knees, and from there it can only spill with senile strength into the cold lower parts of my legs" (D1, p. 160). The drawings of men that Kafka made depicted them as being very tall and skinny.[2]

2. We asked Dr. Leonard Blank of Rutgers University, an authority on the interpretation of human figure drawings, to tell us something about the person (Kafka) who made the three drawings which appear in the second volume of the *Diaries*. These drawings will be found between pages 78 and 79, 144 and 145, and 222 and 223. (This request was made before additional Kafka drawings were included in a new edition of *The Trial*, 1969). Photocopies of the three drawings omitting any identifying information were sent to Dr. Blank who did not recognize them as being the work of Kafka.

Dr. Blank said the person who made the drawings was creative and of high intellect, ambitious yet sees self as warm and ingratiating, somewhat inadequate, striving and energetic yet holds self aloof, and cautious. He bends over backward to please while still managing to achieve his goal. There is a mixture of grandiosity and self-disparagement. He has strong dependency needs and sees women as nurturant. "In summary," Dr. Blank writes, "this is a man of ambivalent identification. A driving individual of humor and competency; he tends to be both ingratiating and dependent while unceasingly pushing to achieve his goals by persuasion, manipulation, or charm."

Although this character sketch brings out traits that are essentially different from (except for the self-disparagement and feelings of inadequacy) but not contradictory to those found in Kafka's dreams, they have, it seems to us, a validity in their own right. That Kafka was creative, of high intellect, and had a sense of humor cannot be denied. Undoubtedly, he was ambitious as a writer and charming, perhaps ingratiating, as a person. He probably had dependency needs with the usual reaction formations against them, and wanted a nurturant woman to replace the lost mother whom he eventually found in Dora Dymant. The only feature that appears not to fit Kafka is "pushing to achieve his goals by persuasion, manipulation, or charm." Instead he tried to achieve his goals as a writer by self-discipline and

Kafka was a little over six feet tall but we have not been able to find out exactly how much he weighed before he became afflicted with tuberculosis although there is little doubt that he was thin. In a letter to Milena written in 1922, two years before he died, he said he weighed 55 kg. (121 pounds). In appearance, Kafka was a good looking, perhaps even handsome man with regular features, dark eyes and hair, and an attractive mouth. Right down to his death, he retained a youthful appearance; at forty, he looked more like a man in his early twenties. Urzidil speaks of Kafka's appearance as being one of "childlike naivité." His boyish looks were responsible for an amusing incident he related to Milena (M, pp. 169–170) when he was about forty. While he was at a swimming pool, one of the employees who was looking for a boy to row a man to a nearby island asked Kafka if he would do it. Kafka proudly complied. Kafka called it "my chief day of glory," and ruefully observes, "Every evening since then I've been waiting in the swimming school for another passenger, but so far no one has shown up" (p. 170). There was nothing feminine or soft about his physical appearance, however. Although definitely not a mesomorph like his father, Kafka was nevertheless manly looking, and he was considered attractive by women and was popular with men. He looked more like the lawyer that he was than like the stereotype of an artist.

Kafka worried continuously about his health. In his diaries he mentioned suffering from a wide range of ailments including constipation, indigestion, insomnia, falling hair, headaches, and curvature of the spine. Brod testified that "Kafka was always very sensitive over the question of any risk to his health. Every imperfection of the body tormented him, even, for example, scurf

---

hard work. It is possible he may have used persuasion, manipulation, or ingratiation in pursuing his activities in the Accident Insurance Institute but of this we have no certain information.

[dandruff], or constipation, or a toe that was not properly formed" (B, p. 108).

Unlike many hypochondriacs, however, Kafka distrusted drugs and doctors. "He demanded that Nature herself should restore the balance, and despised all 'unnatural' medicines" (B, p. 108). Kafka was a vegetarian, drank no alcohol, took cold showers, wore light clothing even in cold weather, and slept with the windows open all year round. He was interested in the nudist movement and in nature cures. For exercise, he walked, swam, rowed, and rode horseback. Brod said Kafka was "outdoorish" and was "passionately interested in sports." Yet in spite of these health measures, he was sickly and eventually developed tuberculosis. Why? Because "[I] have allowed myself to become a physical wreck" (D2, p. 194). "[I have] systematically destroyed myself" (D2, p. 195). One wonders, in the light of these conflicting statements, whether Kafka's interest in health was a reaction formation to a deep-seated aversion to his own body. Why else should he have destroyed himself?

If there was such an aversion, its origin seems to lie in childhood when Kafka compared his frail body with that of his father's (LF, p. 21). The senior Kafka was a large muscular man and made a strong impression upon his only surviving son. The father in turn appeared to have rejected his son because he failed to develop into a sturdy masculine person. That Kafka admired his father's body and was ashamed of his own puny one is poignantly expressed in the *Letter to His Father*.

I remember, for instance, how we often undressed in the same bathing hut. There was I, skinny, weakly, slight; you strong, tall, broad. Even inside the hut I felt a miserable specimen, and what's more, not only in your eyes but in the eyes of the whole world, for you were for me the measure of all things. But then when we stepped out of the bathing hut before the people, you holding me by my hand, a little skeleton, unsteady, barefoot on the boards, frightened of the water, incapable of copying your swimming strokes, which you, with the best of intentions, but actually to my profound humiliation, always kept on showing me, then I was frantic with desperation, and at such moments all my bad experiences in all spheres fitted magnificently together (LF, pp. 19–21).

Kafka then observes that "this difference between us remains much the same to this very day" [1919]. "I was crushed by the mere existence of your body." There are many references in his diaries to the strong bodies of other males.

Kafka stayed at a nudist camp in 1912. He was the only one there who wore swimming trunks. "I am called the man in the swimming trunks" (D2, p. 303). He felt nauseated at the sight of so many naked bodies (p. 305), but he makes references to tall, handsome, sunburned male bodies (p. 306). He also mentions a lecture by the camp doctor in which he describes "a certain exercise [that] will make the sexual organs grow" (p. 303). That Kafka chose to record this particular detail in his diary suggests he may have felt this part of his body was deficient. There is no information in the diaries or biographies on this subject. Kafka evaluated other parts of his body but omitted any mention of his genitals. Nor is it the sort of information that a biographer usually gives even though Brod was surely in a position to know or guess at it. Politzer (1962) makes a reference to Kafka's distrust of his virility (p. 197). Such distrust ofter refers specifically to the size of the genitals, although Politzer may have had other features and traits in mind. Brod (1963) also speaks of "a certain temporary mistrust of his sexual capacity" (p. 37). We have already seen that penis envy manifested itself in one of his dreams (No. 22). In any case, not too much should be made of Kafka's reference to the doctor's prescribed exercise since this is a topic that is of interest to most males however large or small their penis may be. Some reflections on the place of the castration complex in Kafka's personality will be offered in a later chapter.

Kafka's specific feelings about the body seem to have been that (1) he was ashamed of his own body and had an aversion to it, (2) he worried about physical imperfections, and (3) he was both repelled and attracted by the naked bodies of other men.

BODY DISFIGUREMENT

The theme of disfigurement which appeared in seven of Kafka's thirty-seven dreams is a part of the pattern of concern with the body. There are many references to physical deformities in the diaries, and as Brod observed "every imperfection of the body tormented him."

In five of the seven disfigurement dreams, the disfigured person is a female. In at least one of these dreams the relation to sexual disease is fairly clear-cut. In this dream, Kafka was horrified by a whore with a skin rash, particles of which rubbed off on his fingers. One could attribute this dream to fear of venereal disease but it is more than that. By his own admission, Kafka associated sex with filth (LF, p. 105)—also his remark to Janouch, ". . . love always appears hand in hand with filth" (Janouch, 1953, p. 102)—and had few sexual contacts. In a letter to Milena written late in his life, Kafka recounted his first sexual experience with a woman. Of it, he said he was relieved that "the whole experience hadn't been *more* horrible, *more* obscene" (M, p. 163). Yet he ever afterwards regarded this first girl as a "bitter enemy."

I won't say that the sole reason for my enmity was the fact . . . that at the hotel the girl in all innocence had made a tiny repulsive gesture . . . had uttered a trifling obscenity, but the memory remained—I knew at that instant that I would never forget it and simultaneously I knew, that this repulsiveness and smut, though outwardly not necessary, was inwardly however very necessarily connected with the whole thing, and that just this repulsiveness and obscenity . . . had drawn me with such terrible power into this hotel, which otherwise I would have avoided with all my remaining strength (M, p. 164).

Brod said that Kafka "never told a dirty story or even stood for one being told in his presence" (B, p. 116).

For Kafka, then, the body—his body—was not only weak but it was also obscene. "At a certain point in self-knowledge . . . it will invariably follow that you will find yourself execrable. This filth is the nethermost depth you will find" (D2, p. 114). "I'm dirty, Milena, infinitely dirty, which is why I make so much fuss about purity" (M, pp. 185–86).

CLOTHING AND NUDITY

If the body is frail, disfigured, and obscene, then it should be kept covered. Kafka's concern with clothing in his dreams was reflected in his waking life. There are so many detailed descriptions in his diaries of what people were wearing that it would be merely tedious to document them here. Brod comments on Kafka's "elegant suits, which were mostly dark blue . . . as unobtrusive and reserved as himself" (B, p. 43). Photographs of Kafka (Anonymous, 1966) bear out Brod's observation that Kafka, even in informal snapshots, was well dressed. Referring to *The Castle*, Politzer (1962) says "a very important role is assigned to people's clothing . . ." (pp. 222–23).[3] We have already noted Kafka's attitudes toward nudity—his own and others.

SCOPTOPHILIA

It was established that Kafka was a spectator in his dreams. He was also a spectator in waking life. To Janouch, he remarked, "I am an Eye-man" (p. 88). A writer is usually a careful observer.

3. Kafka's interest in clothing may also have been reinforced by the fact that his father was in the wholesale clothing business. Kafka often worked in his father's warehouse.

Kafka's simple but precise descriptions of people, settings, and events have often been commented upon. Brod said that precision and love of detail were prominent features in Kafka's make-up. Kafka liked to attend the theater, to walk through the streets of Prague, and to travel on holidays in foreign countries—all of them predominantly "looking" activities. He did not enjoy music because it was too sensual, producing "dangerous pleasures" (Janouch, 1953, p. 83). He did not like the cinema because the pictures moved too rapidly for him to take them in. Even Kafka's reading preferences—biographies, autobiographies, diaries, and published letters—express an interest in looking into the lives of people. The type of work that Kafka performed in the Worker's Accident Insurance Institute consisted primarily of "looking into" the causes of accidents and the amount of risk involved in the various trades (B, p. 82).

PASSIVITY

Easily the most outstanding feature of Kafka's dreams is the passivity which he displayed in them. There is a low incidence of sex and aggression. The aggression which is expressed is more often verbal than physical, and Kafka was more likely to watch others being aggressive than he was to engage in hostile encounters. This is in line with the general tendency for him to be a spectator rather than a participant in his dreams. His involvement in activities, in contrast to the activities of other dream characters, is significantly lower than the norms. Finally, there is a lower incidence of implements and travel objects in his dreams, categories which are usually associated with activity. The only piece of evidence that runs counter to the passive mode is that when Kafka did engage in an aggression he was more often the aggressor than the victim, which is contrary to the norms.

There is an abundance of evidence to indicate that Kafka was a passive person. Brod says he was entirely lacking in push (B, p. 78). He characterized himself in his letter to his father as being weak, timid, hesitant, and lacking in confidence—qualities which were the opposite of those he perceived in his masterful father. Kafka's pathetic indecisiveness which amounted almost to a pathological state of abulia is vividly described by Milena in a letter to Brod.

Have you ever gone to the post office with him? After he has filed away a telegram and then, shaking his head, picked out the window he likes best, and after he has tramped from one window to the next, without in the least understanding why and wherefore until he finally stumbles on the right one, and after he has paid and received his change—he counts up what he has received, finds that he has been given a crown too much, and returns the crown to the girl at the window. Then he walks slowly away, counts his change again, and on the last step down to the street he sees that the returned crown did belong to him after all. Now you stand helplessly beside him—he shifts his weight from one foot to the other and ponders what he ought to do . . . (B, pp. 227–28).

Milena says this is repeated in every shop, in every restaurant, in front of every beggar.

In his diaries, he saw himself as "a person lost in himself beyond hope of rescue" (D2, p. 11). There are many references to resting, sleeping or not sleeping, malaise, and suicide, and to the emptiness, loneliness, and meaninglessness of life. He stated he would meet death with contentment.

Kafka may have been passive but he was no misanthrope in his public life, according to Max Brod, who said of Kafka that he was good fun, had a joyful nature and a positive attitude toward life, and was interested in everything. He had a wide circle of friends whom he visited and who visited him. He was not a talker, says Brod, preferring to remain silent and listen. Urzidil (1959) quotes Thieberger, a friend of Kafka's, as saying that Kafka was "less active than reactive" in conversation. "That observation," Urzidil states, "hits the nail on the head. Kafka never deliberately imposed his ideas upon anyone but rather waited quietly for the other fellow to take the initiative" (p. 101). (He seems, however, to have talked a great deal with Janouch and even to have imposed his views on his young friend.) Urzidil also describes Kafka's behavior at a public performance as sneaking in unobtrusively and standing in a corner.

He was popular with his fellow workers but he was considered to be the "office baby." He was interested in politics and reform measures but he was never a political activist.

The strongest indication of Kafka's passivity or inertia is the kind of life he led. He never married but lived most of his life in his parents' home. He worked for years as a clerk in a quasi-governmental insurance association. He often found it difficult to write and his three novels were never completed. His favorite pastimes were reading, attending the theater and lectures, sight-seeing, and walking. His physical activities were of the noncompetitive type—swimming, rowing, and horseback riding. He had few sexual relationships although he confessed late in his life that "sex keeps gnawing, hounds me day and night" (D2, p. 203). There is no evidence of his having been physically aggressive in his waking life.

With regard to passivity, then, the congruence between his dreams and behavior is striking.

ATTITUDES TOWARD HIS FATHER

In two dreams, Kafka expressed direct hostility toward his father, in another he resented the fact that his father did not help him scale a wall, and in the fourth dream in which his father appeared, he revealed a deep-seated, almost umbilical attachment to his father. It should be pointed out, however, that the incidence of Kafka dreaming about his father does not exceed the norm for males approximately of his age.

Ambivalence of a son for his father is not unusual, either in dreams or waking life, but in Kafka's case this ambivalence seems to have been particularly crippling. The evidence is set forth in great detail in Kafka's letter to his father. For those readers who are not familiar with the contents of this letter, a few quotations may help to convey its general tenor.

From your armchair you ruled the world. Your opinion was correct, every other was mad. . . . For me you took on the enigmatic quality that all tyrants have whose rights are based on their person and not on reason (LF, p. 21).

It was enough that I should take a little interest in a person— which in any case did not happen often, as a result of my nature —for you, without any consideration for my feelings or respect for my judgment, to move in with abuse, defamation, and denigration (LF, p. 25).

At table one wasn't allowed to do anything but eat, but you cleaned and cut your fingernails, sharpened pencils, cleaned your ears with a toothpick (LF, p. 27).

Rather, the nervous heart condition is a means by which you exert your domination more strongly, since the thought of it necessarily chokes off the least opposition from others. This is, of course, not a reproach, only a statement of fact (LF, p. 31).

When I began to do something you did not like and you threatened me with the prospect of failure, my veneration for your opinion was so great that the failure became inevitable, even though perhaps it happened only at some later time (LF, p. 37).

You have a particularly beautiful, very rare way of quietly, contentedly, approvingly smiling, a way of smiling that can make the person for whom it is meant entirely happy (LF, p. 43).

It is clear from the letter and from other evidence that Kafka loved, hated, admired, and feared his father. He blamed him for being a bad father, but he also blamed himself for being an unworthy son. Kafka believed his father prevented him from becoming an independent, self-reliant person. Marriage "was barred to me because it is your very own domain" (LF, p. 115). Even when Kafka felt he had achieved some independence from his father, he employed the following analogy to express the consequence: it was "reminiscent of the worm that, when a foot treads on its tail end, breaks loose with its front part and drags itself aside" (LF, p. 85).

Brod said that Kafka rarely spoke to his father in later years which is confirmed by Kafka. "[I] hardly ever said more than hello to my father" (D1, p. 300). Janouch recounts an incident in which he and Kafka were walking past the senior Kafka's place of business. The father emerged from the warehouse and yelled very loudly, "Franz. Go home. The air is damp." "Kafka said, in a strangely gentle voice: 'My father. He is anxious about me. Love often wears the face of violence.'" (Janouch, 1953, p. 31). In this instance, however, Kafka may have been inventing an excuse for his father's crude conduct in the presence of a third person.

ATTITUDES TOWARD WOMEN

Kafka's mother appeared in only one of his dreams and only in a subordinate role. This is unusual since in male dreams the mother is represented as often as the father. According to the norm, she would have appeared in four of Kafka's dreams. Why she did not may be explained on the basis of conflicting assumptions regarding dreams. One may assume that the failure of a character or any other dream element to be adequately represented is due to repression. The subject matter is too "hot" to come into dream consciousness. Or one may assume that the character is no longer or never was a conflictful figure for the dreamer. There is a third possibility, that the dream element is represented in a displaced or symbolic guise, and not in its original form. Finally, it is possible that Kafka did not write down the dreams in which his mother was a central character.

We do not have sufficient evidence to confirm or to reject any of these hypotheses. We do know, however, that Kafka did express ambivalence toward other women in his dreams. The incidence of Kafka's aggressive and friendly interactions with females is almost the same, whereas in the normative male group, friendliness toward women exceeds aggression. We have also observed ambivalence in his dreams about Milena.

That Kafka was ambivalent toward women in waking life is clearly evident. We have already seen his aversion to sex. He had a long drawn out love affair with a Berlin woman, Felice Bauer, which was marked by extreme mood swings. They were engaged, the engagement broken, engaged again, and again broken. It must have been a tormenting relationship for both parties. Later, there was a similar affair with another woman, to be followed by his ambivalent relationship with Milena. During the period of the Milena affair, Kafka commented to Janouch, "Women are snares, which lie in wait for men on all sides in order to drag them into the merely finite. They lose their dangers if one voluntarily falls into one of the snares. But if, as a result of habit, one overcomes it, then all the jaws of the female trap open again" (Janouch, 1953, pp. 101–2). And he writes in his diary July 21, 1913, "Copulation is punishment for the happiness of living together." It is of interest that Kafka's conception of Utopia was a society of single men, from which married men and all women were excluded (B, p. 85). It was not until the end of his life when he met Dora Dymant that he seems to have found a satisfying association with a woman other than his favorite sister, Ottla.

THE MASCULINIZED WOMAN

There is another feature of Kafka's dreams regarding women

which is peculiar. This is the theme of the masculinized woman. We believe that the presence of this unusual theme is an important key for understanding Kafka's behavior. Why did Kafka conceive of women as being masculine? There may be a number of reasons for this attitude but we would like to direct our attention to one which is especially relevant in the light of Kafka's waking behavior. We believe that Kafka identified his mother with his father. In his eyes, she was in league with his father. His mother, consequently, was the prototype of the masculinized woman.

There is considerable evidence to support this hypothesis. Max Brod observed that Kafka felt his parents formed a common bond against him (B, p. 30). During Kafka's childhood, his mother left the house in the morning to help her husband in his business. In the evenings, the father monopolized his wife's time in playing cards. Photographs of Mrs. Kafka show a strong almost hard face and a stalwart figure, made all the more impressive by the fashions of the times (Anonymous, 1966, photographs on pp. 13, 17, 31, 86, 87). She probably resembled the mannish woman who appeared in Dream 8. But it is from Kafka's own lips that we hear the clearest expression of his feelings toward his mother. In 1913, he wrote, "I have not spoken an average of twenty words a day to my mother these last years" (D1, p. 299). Later in the same year he records why he rarely spoke to her. "How furious I am with my mother. I need only begin to talk to her and I am irritated, almost scream" (p. 317).

It is in relation to his father that Kafka's mother is most explicitly defined. In 1916, he wrote in his diary, "Father from one side, Mother from the other, have inevitably almost broken my spirit" (D2, p. 168). In his letter to his father, he defined the situation precisely and clearly.

If I was to escape from you, I had to escape from the family as well, even from Mother. True, one could always get protection from her, but only in relation to you. She loved you too much and was too devoted and loyal to you to have been for long an independent spiritual force in the child's struggle. This was, incidentally, a correct instinct of the child, for with the passing of the years Mother became ever more closely allied to you; . . . she did more and more completely, emotionally rather than intellectually, blindly adopt your judgments and your condemnations with regard to the children (LF, p. 59).

It is true that Mother was illimitably good to me, but for me all that was in relation to you, that is to say in no good relation. *Mother unconsciously played the role of beater during a hunt.* Even if your method of upbringing might in some unlikely case have set me on my own feet by means of producing defiance, dislike, or even hate in me, Mother cancelled that out again by kindness, by talking sensibly . . . by pleading with me; and I was again driven back into your orbit, which I might perhaps otherwise have broken out of, to your advantage and to my own (LF, pp. 45 and 47, emphasis supplied).

It would be difficult to find a more cruel metaphor for a mother's role than "beater during a hunt." He saw his mother flushing him out into the open in order that his father might finish him off.

Since Kafka regarded his mother and father as fellow conspirators, it is small wonder that he perceived women as being masculine. We will return to this very important aspect of Kafka's feelings in a subsequent chapter.

SUMMARY

In this chapter we have examined Kafka's waking behavior in relation to a number of prominent themes in his dreams. A great deal of congruence was found. Kafka in his dreams seems to have been in many respects the same person he was when he was awake. Our first objective, to show continuities in behavior between sleeping and waking life, has been realized.

Were dreams merely a reflection of waking life, there would be little to be gained by analyzing dreams since one could obtain the same information by observing waking behavior. It is our contention, however, that dreams illuminate much that may be obscure about the underlying motives for a person's behavior in waking life. Dreams shed light on the unconscious dynamics of personality to an extent that is probably unmatched by any other type of material.

We will attempt to exemplify this thesis by showing how the various features of Kafka's dreams fit together and help to account for the sort of person Kafka was. Before doing this, however, we shall present the results of an analysis of some of Kafka's writings using the same methods that were used in analyzing his dreams. This is being done in order to demonstrate the relationship between material in his dreams and another important sector of his behavior, namely, his work as a writer.

Our analysis of Kafka's writings will be restricted to the three novels, *Amerika*, *The Trial*, and *The Castle* because they, unlike the short stories and parables, provide a wealth of behavioral data about a single character, the protagonist of each novel. Our principal objective in this chapter is to show how Kafka portrayed the protagonists—Karl Rossmann in *Amerika*, Joseph K. in *The Trial*, and K. in *The Castle*—in his relations with males and females, and with authorities and nonauthorities. We shall use these data to help expand our knowledge of some of the material in Kafka's dreams, to examine congruences between his dreams, life, and writings, and to aid us in arriving at a formulation of some aspects of Kafka's personality. It also illustrates the application to literature of a system of content analysis which we have found useful in analyzing dreams.

Before presenting the results of our analysis, we would like to make some observations on the relation of a writer's life and personality to his writings in order to clarify the limits of this study. The writing of fiction is, of course, a form of expressive behavior. The fiction writer expresses his thoughts and feelings about himself, about other people, and about the world in the stories he tells. He may or may not be fully aware of the ideas and attitudes he is trying to express and he may or may not be fully aware of his reasons for selecting the particular incidents that go to make up the story. Writers do not usually examine their motives publicly or provide a commentary on what they write. Kafka was no exception to this rule. Lacking this information it is hazardous for the reader or critic to form any judgment as to the role that the unconscious plays in the creation of a particular work of fiction.

In this post-Freudian era, it is usually conceded that the creative writer is distinguished from the bulk of mankind by being in closer touch with his unconscious. Instead of repressing feelings and ideas, he accepts them and expresses them through the medium of literature. What this means is that the writer has succeeded in bringing into the preconscious where it is available much of what remains irretrievably unconscious for most people. In Kafka's case, this seems to be quite evident.[1] Not only was he extremely observant, introspective, thoughtful, and analytical, as his diaries and letters reveal, but he also took great pains to express the complexities and paradoxes of human existence, which he discovered in himself, as truthfully as possible. Because the conditions of human existence are far from simple, Kafka's stories are extremely recondite in spite of his precise narrative style and his vocabulary of common, everyday words.

Metamorphosis, for instance, is a straightforward story of the experiences of a man who turns into a bug. It is absorbing, entertaining, humorous, pathetic, lucidly written, and completely realized. It is acknowledged to be one of the great short stories in literature. Why then do we need to be told what it is about as scores of critics have attempted to do? The answer is that it is assumed there are hidden meanings—a latent content—behind the outward appearance of the story. It is not simply a story about a man who turns into a bug; it is an allegory which requires interpretation in the same way that a dream requires interpretation if its meaning is to be grasped.

Our intention is not to tell what each of Kafka's three novels is about either on a manifest or a latent level. The method of content analysis we have employed merely describes quantitatively some of the interactions among the characters. The categories that were selected were some of the same ones that had

1. Urzidil (1968) is of the opinion that although Kafka was acquainted with Freud and even better acquainted with Goethe "as the most decisive proclaimer of the significance of the unconscious," he did not need either of them as mentors. "The reactions issuing forth from the unconscious constitute the pith and substance of his most characteristic satire" (p. 61).

been found to be significant in Kafka's dreams and in his life. We were interested to see whether this type of analysis of Kafka's novels might generate data that would support inferences drawn from the analysis of Kafka's dreams and his life. In pursuing this objective we also turned up other data which we feel extends our understanding of Kafka's personality particularly with respect to some developmental changes.

The Castle

Our analysis began with *The Castle*. We will limit the analysis to friendly and aggressive interactions between the hero and two groups of characters, those who wield some authority by virtue of their position and those who have no authority. Characters who held positions of authority in the Village or Castle, and with whom K. had some form of aggressive or friendly inter-action, were the following:

Males:
> Landlord of the Bridge Inn
> Landlord of the Herrenhof Inn
> Teacher
> Superintendent of the Village
> Klamm, an official of the Castle
> Erlanger, one of Klamm's chief secretaries
> Momus, Klamm's Village secretary
> Oswald, an official of the Castle
> Schwarzer, son of a Castle official

Females:
> Landlady of the Bridge Inn
> Landlady of the Herrenhof Inn
> Gisa, a teacher

Scales devised by Hall and Van de Castle (1966a) to score aggression and friendliness were used. The aggression scale, it will be recalled, consists of such items as assault, destructiveness, theft, coercion, rejection, quarreling, and feelings of hostility. A character who initiates the aggression is called the aggressor, the object of the aggression is called the victim. The friendliness scale includes such items as rendering a service, inviting, visiting, giving a present, greeting, and feelings of friendliness. It also includes physical acts of a friendly but nonsexual nature, e.g., shaking hands. We also scored sexual interactions of which there were five but none of these was with an authority. They were added to the total number of friendly interactions.

We read through the Penguin edition of *The Castle* (1957) and scored every aggressive and friendly interaction in which K. was involved with any character whatsoever. There was a total of 86 aggressions and 75 friendlinesses. Of the 86 aggressions, 21 were between K. and male authorities, and 18 were between K. and female authorities. Of the 75 friendly interactions, 7 were between K. and male authorities and 4 between K. and female authorities.

Since the number of aggressive and friendly encounters with male and female authorities may depend both upon the total number of authorities of each sex in *The Castle* and upon the number and length of the contacts between K. and each authority, a proportion was computed which eliminates the influence of these two factors. The proportion is obtained by dividing the number of aggressions K. has with a given class of character by the number of aggressions *plus* the number of friendly encounters K. has with the class. Out of the 28 friendly and aggressive encounters K. has with male authorities, 21 of them are aggressive. This yields a proportion of .75. The proportion for female authorities is .82 (18/22). These two proportions are not significantly different and show that K. is involved in many more aggressive than friendly interactions with *both* male and female authorities.

It is necessary, however, to demonstrate by a statistical analysis that there are more aggressions with male and female authorities than would be expected by chance. The expected proportion is obtained by dividing the total number of aggressions K. has with all characters by the total number of aggressions and friendliness. This proportion is .53 (86/161). The combined proportion for male and female authorities is .78. The difference between these two proportions is significant at the .01 level.

Having established that K. has many more aggressive than friendly encounters with authorities of both sexes, let us now see who initiates the aggression more often, K. or the authorities. Of those aggressions in which an aggressor and a victim could be identified, K. is the victim of male authorities 13 out of 18 times (.72) and he is the victim of female authorities 15 out of 16 times (.94). With all characters in *The Castle* K. is the victim 47 times and the aggressor 35 times which yields a proportion of victim/victim + aggressor of .57. This was used as the expected proportion. The difference between this expected proportion and the one obtained for male and female authorities combined .82 (28/34) is significant at the .01 level. This finding clearly establishes that K. is more often the victim of aggression by both male and female authorities than he is the aggressor.

The foregoing results hold not only for male and female authority figures in general but they are also true of K's interactions with most of the individual authority figures. The four authorities with whom K. has the most interactions and the incidence of K's aggressive and friendly encounters with each of them is as follows:

	AGGRESSIVE	FRIENDLY
Landlady of the Bridge Inn	11	4
Male teacher	6	2
Landlady of the Herrenhof Inn	4	1
Landlord of the Bridge Inn	2	3

The only exception is the Bridge Inn landlord with whom K. has more friendly than aggressive interactions.

We then made the same type of analysis of K's interactions with persons who did not hold positions of authority.

Among the most ubiquitous characters in *The Castle* are Arthur and Jeremiah, K's two assistants. Like K's interactions with authorities there is a preponderance of aggressions relative to friendliness with the assistants, .77 (17/22), but unlike his interactions with authorities, K. is, with only one exception, the aggressor. The one exception comes at the end of the book when the assistants finally rebel against K's ill treatment of them.

Who the assistants represent in Kafka's life—if they represent anyone—is not clear. They may represent his sisters, his deceased brothers, or the rebellious side of Kafka's personality. Neider (1962) notes that Kafka often uses two persons or two objects in his writings. There are two assistants, two inns, two sisters in *The Castle*; two warders and two executioners in *The Trial*; two mechanics and two information givers in *Amerika*; two bouncing balls, two girls, and two assistants in the short story, *Blumfeld*. Neider says, "I have counted 33 separate uses of the number two in *Amerika*, 51 in *The Trial*, 44 in *The Castle*, and many in the shorter fiction." In a burst of enthusiasm for what he imagines to be a Freudian interpretation, Neider identifies the two assistants in *The Castle* as testicles and deficient sexuality. Neider's principal thesis is that Kafka deliberately used "Freudian" symbols in his writings. Whatever the assistants may symbolize, K.

treats them as scapegoats on whom he can vent his frustrations arising from his vain attempts to find acceptance in the Village or by the Castle authorities.

Inspired by Neider, we counted the incidence of the number two in Kafka's dreams and found there were twelve. In Dream 8, there are two pillars and two critics, in Dream 10 two entrances, in Dream 13 two groups of sunbathers, in Dream 22 two friends and two hands, in Dream 24 two little loops on his father's bathrobe, in Dream 25 two groups of men, in Dream 29 two fingers, and in Dream 33 two first and two last sentences, and two dresses. This does not seem to be an inordinate use of the number two nor does the context in which the number appears suggest any consistent symbolic interpretation. It would be difficult to make a case for a common meaning for two pillars, two critics, two entrances, two hands, two sentences, and two dresses, although it is possible that each of these has its own individual symbolic significance.

Another group of characters with whom K. has many interactions are six individuals who have no official connection with either the Village or the Castle. Two are males, Barnabas and Hans, and four are females, Frieda, Pepi, and Barnabas' sisters, Olga and Amelia. Although Barnabas is a messenger in the employ of the Castle he has few if any official duties or responsibilities. Hans is a village schoolboy who feels sorry for K. The four young women are all more or less in love with K. but only Frieda becomes his lover. He has four sexual interactions with Frieda and one abortive one with Pepi. Except for Hans, who is younger, these characters are much the same age as K. K. has many more friendly than aggressive interactions with them. The proportion, aggressions/aggressions + friendlinesses, is .21 (3/14) for Barnabas and Hans, and .24 (13/54) for the four young women. The proportion for the two sexes combined is .23 (16/68) which is significantly different from the expected proportion of .53. In the aggressive encounters, K. is aggressor and victim equally often (8 versus 8), and in the friendly encounters he is befriender and befriended with almost the same frequency (25 versus 23).

These findings show that K's pattern of aggression and friendliness with authorities differs markedly from the pattern with the assistants, and this pattern differs from the one with peer males and females. K. is the victim of considerable hostility from Village and Castle authorities, abuses his assistants, and has friendly relations with peer males and females.

What do these findings mean in relation to the information obtained from an analysis of Kafka's dreams and waking life behavior? If it is assumed that the authority figures in *The Castle* are surrogates for Kafka's parents, then the results support the thesis that Kafka felt his mother and father were in league against him. Two pairs of authorities—the landlords and landladies of the two inns—are husbands and wives. The male and female teachers, although not married to each other, act more or less in unison in their hostility toward K. Whether consciously or unconsciously, Kafka projected into the writing of *The Castle* conceptions of his parents. Life and literature merge at this point. The theme of the masculinized woman in the dreams is represented in *The Castle* by the female authorities who are as hostile to K. as the male authorities are. In fact, the most hostile character is the landlady of the Bridge Inn.

Let us now look at the results obtained by making a similar analysis of *Amerika* and *The Trial*. Although neither of these earlier novels yields the same pattern of social interactions found in *The Castle*, they reveal a very interesting development in Kafka's conception of the hero's relations with various classes of people. In *Amerika*, people are, with several exceptions, friendly and helpful to Karl. It is largely a benign world except that Karl fails to take advantage of it. In *The Trial,* Joseph K. is aggressive toward the other characters but despite his hostility he receives a lot of friendliness from them. We will consider the implications of these generalizations after presenting the data upon which they are based.

Amerika

In *Amerika,* Karl is involved in more friendly than aggressive interactions, 194 versus 125. The proportion, aggressions divided by the sum of aggressions and friendliness, is .41. The proportion for Karl's encounters with male characters is .45, and for female characters the proportion is .29. Out of 96 encounters with female characters only 28 of them are aggressive.

Karl is more often the victim than the aggressor, 80 versus 45, and more often befriended than the befriender, 118 versus 76. The proportions do not differ significantly for encounters with male and female characters. In other words, Karl is the recipient of both aggression and friendliness, but there is more of the latter than of the former.

The male authorities in *Amerika* divide into two categories: those who are hostile to Karl and those who are helpful. The first category consists of Karl's two "bosses"—the Head Porter and the Head Waiter—in the hotel where he works for a short time. Out of 22 encounters with them, 19 are unfriendly, and in all of these 19 Karl is the victim. The second category consists of older men, e.g., Karl's uncle and his uncle's friend, Pollander. With them Karl has few aggressive interactions (the proportion is .25), and he is the recipient of considerable friendliness from them (the proportion is .71).

The only female authority with whom Karl interacts is the Manageress of the hotel. She is almost always friendly to Karl, 19 friendly versus 2 unfriendly. So is Therese, a fellow employee, and Karl is also friendly to her. The situation is quite different for Karl's social interactions with another peer female, Clara. With her he has more hostile relations, 15 aggressions versus six friendly. In these encounters, there is a give and take although Clara is more apt to be the aggressor, nine aggressions against Karl versus six by Karl against her. Moreover, her aggressions are more violent and physical than his. She is a "masculine" woman. It is interesting that Karl's relations with Mr. Mack, Clara's fiance, are exclusively friendly.

The analysis so far shows that there are good "father" figures who try to help the immigrant boy who has been sent to the United States by his parents for having made a servant girl pregnant, and bad "father" figures who are cruel to Karl. Peer females are also divided into friendly and hostile types but the one "mother" figure is almost uniformly helpful. Spilka (1963) observes that the Manageress and the Chief Waiter are in league against Karl and that this reflects Kafka's feelings about his own mother and father. It is true that after befriending Karl the Manageress lets him be discharged but the charges against Karl are so serious that she cannot overlook them.

Several characters do not fit the foregoing analysis. One of these is the Stoker on the ship by which Karl travels to New York. Karl befriends him eight times—there is no hostility—but the Stoker is ambivalent toward Karl, five aggressions and five friendlinesses toward Karl.

The pattern of aggression and friendliness with the two mechanics, Delamarche and Robinson, whom Karl meets on the road and with whom he travels, and later lives, and with Brunelda, Delamarche's mistress, are also different from the other characters in the book. With these three characters, Karl has 55 aggressive and 45 friendly interactions. Karl is the aggressor

29 times and the victim 26 times. He is the befriender 16 times and he is befriended 29 times. These characters like the others in the book except for Clara and the Stoker befriend Karl, but they also give and receive a lot of aggression.

In contrast to *The Castle* in which the main characters can be grouped in three classes—hostile authorities, mistreated assistants, and friendly peers—the characters in *Amerika* constitute a number of types. There are two groups of male authorities—one friendly, the other hostile—one friendly female authority and one friendly peer female, one unfriendly and masculine peer female, one befriended male who is ambivalent toward Karl, and three characters with whom Karl has ambivalent relations. What Kafka appears to have done in this early novel is to split up his ambivalent feelings about people, especially male authorities and peer females, and project them onto different characters.

The Trial

In *The Trial* as in *Amerika*, Joseph K. has the same pattern of aggression and friendliness with both authorities and nonauthorities. With the male characters, Joseph K. has more aggressive than friendly interactions (131 versus 96), and with female characters he has more friendly than aggressive interactions (73 versus 39).

In his aggressive interactions, Joseph K. is more often the aggressor than the victim (120 versus 64) which differs markedly from the same analysis for *Amerika*. This is true for both male and female characters. With regard to friendliness, Joseph K. is more often befriended by others than he befriends them (108 versus 63). In other words, people are friendly toward Joseph K. but he is aggressive toward them. For example, Huld, Joseph K's lawyer, is aggressed against nine times by his client and is never treated in a friendly manner by Joseph K. Huld is aggressive only three times and he is friendly seven times. Hostility to and from Leni, Huld's nurse, occurs twelve and nine times respectively while she is friendly to Joseph K. fourteen times and he is friendly to her only half as often.

Some characters deviate from the general trend. Joseph K. is friendlier to Fräulein Bürstner than she is to him (nine versus four) but this is because he is trying to seduce her. With one character, Berthold, a law student, Joseph K. has only aggressive interactions and Joseph K. is usually the aggressor (seven versus two). With two characters, a girl whom Joseph K. meets in a courtroom and a manufacturer, he has only friendly encounters. With the painter, Titorelli, there are thirteen friendly interactions, eleven of which are initiated by Titorelli, and only one aggressive encounter.

Uncles appear in both *Amerika* and *The Trial*. In *Amerika*, Karl has thirteen friendly interactions and only one aggression with Uncle Jacob. Most of the friendliness is initiated by the uncle (nine versus four). With the uncle in *The Trial*, Joseph K. has eight aggressive and six friendly interactions. Of the eight aggressions, five are initiated by the uncle, and of the six friendly acts only one is initiated by the nephew. The friendly uncle in *Amerika* becomes an ambivalent uncle in *The Trial*.

There is still a tendency for Kafka to split his ambivalent feelings and project them onto different characters in *The Trial* but it is not as pronounced as in *Amerika*. In one respect, Joseph K's interactions are like those in Kafka's dreams. Kafka is more often the aggressor than the victim in his dreams and Joseph K. is also more often the aggressor than the victim. There is a slight tendency for Kafka to be more often the recipient of friendliness than the initiator in his dreams (eleven versus eight) which is also true for Joseph K.

SUMMARY

Although some parallels have been found between Kafka's dreams and his writings, it is plainly evident that the interactions between the heroes and other characters in the three novels are much more complex than Kafka's social interactions in his dreams. The greater complexity of literature as compared to dreams may be explained as follows. A very creative and imaginative writer such as Kafka has access to a wide range of psychic material which he can work over and rearrange in an infinite number of ways. Awake, the conscious ego is able to employ its capacities for discriminating, selecting, criticizing, reasoning, testing, and positioning experiences in space and time. The writer exercises control over his material in a manner which the dreamer is unable to do. A dream happens to a person; a writer makes his story happen. A dream is unconsciously created whereas a story is consciously created. Although nearly every critic has stressed the dreamlike character of Kafka's writings, they are not dreams but the highly disciplined and refined products of a powerful intellect. Aspiring to be fully conscious, Kafka came as close to that ideal state as it is probably possible to come.

We know from his diaries that Kafka relentlessly explored the "nethermost" depths of his being, and it was these explorations that provided the rich material for his writings. Unlike many writers who are obsessed by a specific complex and who write the same novel over and over again, Kafka apparently had no single neurotic fixation that limited his vision. He made himself aware of much of the human condition with all of its intricacies and ambiguities and he could and did write about them. Spilka (1963) was quite right, we believe, to compare Kafka with Dickens, another writer who ranged over the whole domain of human experience. Spilka stresses Kafka's "childlike sensibility" which, in our opinion, is also correct since the boundary between consciousness and unconsciousness is usually more permeable in children than in adults. Kafka's flexibility is most easily seen in his short stories, no two of which deal with the same theme. It is this universal quality, we believe, that accounts for Kafka's great appeal and influence. There is something in his writings for every reader, and something new is seen every time he is reread. That is why the stories can bear the burden of so many different critical interpretations.

A COMPARISON OF KAFKA'S THREE NOVELS

The following discussion is intended to show by a specific example how a quantitative approach to the analysis of literature can provide data from which important inferences may be drawn. The three novels, *Amerika, The Trial,* and *The Castle,* were written in that order. *Amerika* was begun in 1912, *The Trial* in 1914, and *The Castle* probably in 1921 or 1922. The way in which male and female characters and authorities and nonauthorities were represented in relation to the hero changed from one novel to the next. In all three novels, the hero has more aggressive interactions with males than with females, but the proportion of aggressions relative to the sum of aggressions and friendlinesses between the hero and both sexes increases from *Amerika* to *The Trial* to *The Castle* as the following table shows.

$\dfrac{\text{Aggressions}}{\text{Aggressions + Friendlinesses}}$	Amerika	The Trial	The Castle
Hero with males	.45	.58	.66
Hero with females	.29	.35	.42

When characters are separated into authorities and nonauthorities, the proportion of aggressive encounters with authorities of both sexes increases while the proportion with nonauthorities does not change systematically, as the following table shows.

Aggressions	Amerika	The Trial	The Castle
Aggressions + Friendlinesses			
Hero with male authorities	.47	.67	.75
Hero with female authorities	.07	.29	.82
Hero with male nonauthorities	.29	.50	.21
Hero with female nonauthorities	.37	.37	.24

Especially notable is the large increase in the hero's aggressive encounters with female authorities from a negligible .07 in *Amerika* to .82 in *The Castle*. The latter proportion is not significantly different from the proportion of K's aggressions with male authorities. In *Amerika*, even the "fathers" are more friendly than hostile, although not as friendly as the "mothers"; in *The Castle* both "fathers" and "mothers" are enemies in the eyes of K.

Further light is cast upon Kafka's frame of mind when he wrote each of the novels by considering the analysis of the hero as victim or befriended, and as aggressor or befriender. In *Amerika*, Karl is more often the victim than the aggressor, and more often befriended than the befriender. This is true for his encounters with most of the characters. He receives both aggression and friendliness but there is more of the latter than of the former. In *The Trial*, Joseph K. is more often the aggressor to nearly all types of characters than he is the victim. In spite of his aggressiveness, however, Joseph K. receives a lot of friendliness from many of the characters. A further development takes place in *The Castle*. K. again becomes a victim, but in contrast to Karl in *Amerika*, he is the victim of authorities and not of nonauthorities. Moreover, he is no more likely to be befriended than a befriender.

We may summarize these findings by imputing to Kafka the following views of himself in relation to people. In *Amerika*, he is saying people, generally speaking, are good to me. In *The Trial*, he is still saying people are good to me in spite of my hostility toward them. His final view as expressed in *The Castle* is that his enemies are authorities and his friends are nonauthorities, usually peers. Karl is a trusting child, Joseph K. is a rebellious adolescent, and K. is a more analytical adult. For it is in *The Castle* that he realizes who his chief enemies are, namely, his parents and all parental figures.

Neider (1962) uses Freudian categories to characterize the three novels. *Amerika,* according to this critic, is oral, *The Trial* is anal, and *The Castle* is early genital. "Early genital" is the beginning of the Oedipal period. Our findings substantiate the classification for *Amerika* but not for the other two novels. In *Amerika,* Karl is dependent upon the friendliness ("oral supplies") of others. *The Trial* is not anal according to our analysis because although there is rebellion by the hero (which is an anal trait), there is not a corresponding imposition of prohibitions ("toilet training") by authority figures. Our results more nearly confirm Erich Fromm's (1951) interpretation of Joseph K's character. Fromm says Joseph K. has a receptive orientation; he wants to obtain from others what he desires without giving anything in return except resentment. *The Castle* is not Oedipal in any ordinary sense because K's interactions with female authorities are as hostile as they are with male authorities. *The Castle* does, however, represent Kafka's deviant Oedipal pattern which, as we have noted, is more like that of females than of males.

Hermann Kafka (*upper left*)
Julie Löwy Kafka (*right*)
Franz Kafka (*lower left*)

5. A FORMULATION OF SOME DETERMINANTS OF KAFKA'S PERSONALITY

In the previous chapters, we have stayed fairly close to empirical data and have drawn relatively few inferences from the findings because our objective was to make an empirical investigation of the relationship between dreams and waking behavior. This objective having been reached, we will now pull together the results of our analysis and, with the aid of Freudian theory, formulate some of the primary determinants of Kafka's personality and behavior.

As we observed earlier, Kafka's dreams, as well as his waking behavior, have many similarities to those of other young men. We assume that these similarities are due to universal determinants of the human psyche which have been spelled out so trenchantly in the writings of Freud and Jung.[1] The fact that Kafka's dreams contain universal themes does not, of course, make them any less important. For example, the presence of sadism and masochism in Kafka's make-up is clearly evident in Dreams 25 and 30, respectively. They are found in everyone's dreams. Kafka had to deal with these impulses in waking life, as others do, either by expression, repression, displacement, or reaction formation. There are also oral elements in his dreams but this does not mean that Kafka was an "oral character." It merely tells us that he, like the rest of the human race, passed through an oral stage in his development and that this stage left a residue in his personality. We would assume from Dreams 6 and 11 that he also passed through an anal stage and from Dream 15 that he had a phallic period. One can, if he chooses, treat Kafka as a particular embodiment of Everyman and make out of his dreams a catalogue of the human psyche. Since such a catalogue has

1. Cross-cultural studies of reported dreams are now being undertaken by one of the writers (Hall). Preliminary findings indicate that there are many commonalities in the dreams of people throughout the world.

already been made by Freud and Jung and their followers, it is not necessary to repeat the task here.

Recently, the Associate Director of the New York City Opera, John S. White (1967), examined the relation of personality and tuberculosis using Kafka as his specimen case. He finds in "his patient" such a galaxy of mechanisms, dynamics, and structures that Kafka is metamorphosed into a psychiatric textbook. White is not the first one to have made such a metamorphosis (*vide* Goodman, 1947, and Neider, 1962); he is just the most recent. Moreover, the psychic determinants of tuberculosis are so broad, according to White's analysis, that we should all be victims of the disease.

Our objective, then, is not to find the Everyman in Kafka but to look for some of the determinants that made Kafka the individual he appeared to be. In pursuing this quest, we have been guided by aspects of Freud's libido theory.

According to libido theory, the infant's first libidinal objects are his own body and the mother, or initially the mother's breasts. The body is the original source of narcissistic pleasure and the mother is the baby's first external object with whom he has a libidinal relationship. How the baby experiences his body and his mother is assumed to have far-reaching effects on his subsequent development.

Inevitably, both the body due to hunger, illness, and pain, and the mother due to separation anxiety and punishments become sources of pain as well as of pleasure, so that ambivalence toward each of them is the rule rather than the exception. The degree to which the ambivalence is weighted toward either the positive or negative side is determined by the amount of pleasure or pain that the individual experiences. Too much pain can turn the child against his body or his mother, as the case may be. These negative feelings then generate a lot of side effects which pervade and influence the whole personality. It is our contention that the experiences Kafka had and the fantasies that accompanied or followed these experiences produced in him an unusual degree of aversion to his body and to his mother. These strong aversions gave a unique stamp to his personality and behavior.

KAFKA'S AVERSION TO HIS BODY

The evidence clearly indicates that Kafka had an aversion for his body and for his mother. Why did he have an aversion for his body? Assuming that he was born with a frail constitution, the decisive factors appear to us to be the way in which he compared his body with his father's and the way in which the senior Kafka reacted to his son's physique. Every little boy feels small and weak alongside his father, and these feelings of inferiority persist to some degree throughout life. They are counteracted to a great extent by the boy's identification with the father, an identification which enables him to become a father himself. In Kafka's case feelings of physical inferiority were exacerbated by the father's overt and persistent rejection of his son. Kafka could not establish an identification with his father; therefore he could not become a father.[2]

Kafka's letter to his father reveals how passionately he yearned for such an identification, and how resolutely his father spurned his son. Kafka eventually tried to reach his father through his writings—"my writing was all about you" (LF, p. 85). He dedicated one of his books to his father and when Kafka gave him a copy, his father merely said, "Put it on the table by my bed" (B, p. 31). No contact was ever made. We have already cited the swimming scene with his father and the almost total lack of communication between the two men.

2. Kafka is alleged to have fathered a son according to information received by Max Brod from the mother some years after Kafka's death (B, pp. 240–42). If he was in fact a father it was never known to Kafka.

Physical inferiority, whether fancied or real, often acts as a barrier to the pursuit of normal masculine activities. Sex and aggression are dampened resulting in a passive mode of existence. Getting married, becoming a father, and striving for vocational distinction are blocked. One becomes a spectator watching others do what one would like to do.

Aversion to the body can easily lead to the feeling that the body is dirty. We have already presented evidence from his dreams and from other sources that Kafka regarded the body—his body as well as the bodies of others—as disfigured and obscene.

Nakedness is also associated with violence and lust. In Dream 3, Kafka is playing with the naked body of a diseased whore; in Dream 8, there is a naked disfigured girl; in Dream 9, too much nakedness is displayed in a painting by Ingres; in Dream 13, two groups of sunbathers are fighting; in Dream 22, a sword is withdrawn from Kafka's naked back; and in Dream 25, a naked man is being tortured.

These attitudes toward the naked body would explain the emphasis on clothing in his dreams and in his waking life since clothing hides the body. Elegant attire compensates for an inelegant body. In this connection, Dream 5 is of interest. Kafka is attracted to a man because of the fine clothes he is wearing; even his face is covered by soft material. Naked bodies on the other hand, repelled him.

Much of Kafka's available energy went into his writings; he fathered stories instead of children. But Kafka was even ambivalent about his writing. He complained again and again how hard it was for him to sit down and write. To his father he confessed, "When I rushed away from you, frightfully busy, it was generally in order to lie down in my room" (LF, p. 91). He failed to complete his three novels, and his diaries contain many fragments that are broken off in the middle of a sentence. He was reluctant to have any of his writings appear in print, and the few that appeared during his lifetime were published at the insistence of Brod. "Publication of some scribble of mine always upsets me," Kafka confessed to Janouch (1953, p. 32). He instructed Max Brod to destroy his unpublished manuscripts after his death. Kafka appears to have regarded the corpus of his writings as he did his body—something to be annihilated.

If the body offends, then it should be destroyed. Kafka confessed that he did destroy it (D2, p. 195). The first signs of tuberculosis appeared in 1917 and he died from the disease seven years later. Given his interest in health measures and outdoor activities, the affluence of his family and his own financial security, and the availability of the best methods of treatment in Prague and Vienna, it is difficult to understand why he contracted the disease in the first place and why, when it was diagnosed, effective measures for bringing it under control were not promptly instituted. These considerations lend credence to Kafka's confession that he allowed himself to become a physical wreck.[3]

As might be expected, the eventual wrecking of his body by tuberculosis had many positive aspects for Kafka. Kafka's attitudes toward the disease have been fully documented by White (1967). Kafka referred to it as his "guardian angel"; it was "lovable" and "sweet." "I relate myself to the tuberculosis like a child attached to the apron strings of the mother." Kafka acknowledged that it brought him more good things than bad things. It gave him the excuse that he needed not to marry Felice

3. Brod believes that Kafka's death from tuberculosis was caused by the privation he endured during the winter of 1923–24 when he was living with Dora Dymant in Berlin. Germany was then undergoing its worst period of inflation. Kafka, Brod writes, "stubbornly insists on managing on his tiny pension. Only in the worst case and under great pressure will he accept money and parcels of food from his family" (B, p. 201). Privation may have hastened his death but Kafka's condition had been getting steadily worse during the previous six years.

Bauer or any other woman, although on his deathbed he wished to marry Dora Dymant. It enabled him to live for a while with his favorite sister in the country. Long sick leaves from his job and his eventual retirement gave him more time to write. Most of his major works were written after he became consumptive. And finally it brought him into a close and comforting relationship with a young woman, Dora Dymant, and with a man, Robert Klopstock, a doctor who himself was tubercular. These two—"Franz's little family," as they called themselves—looked after Kafka during his terminal illness.

THE LOST MOTHER

Feelings of physical inferiority account for many of the distinctive features of Kafka's personality and behavior. The other important element that shaped his life, in our opinion, is his feelings about his mother. In his short story *The Married Couple* one of the characters says, "Whatever you say, a mother can do wonders. She puts together again what we have wrecked. *I lost her when I was a child*" (B, p. 30, emphasis supplied). It is our contention that Kafka lost his mother when he was a child, lost her to the masculine world of the father. This would account for the conception of the masculinized woman in his dreams, and the mother and father figures in league against K. in *The Castle*. Politzer (1962) who is not one to delve deeply into a psychological analysis of Kafka or his writings observes that Kafka had "deep rooted aggressions against the maternal principle" (p. 141). These aggressions were, in our opinion, a reflex to early desertion of Kafka by his mother.

The image of a masculinized mother probably also led him to fall in love with forceful women like Felice Bauer and Milena Jesenská. His mother may also have been the model for the strong, dominant, sometimes overpowering female characters in his novels, women like Clara, the hotel Manageress, and Brunelda in *Amerika*, Fräulein Bürstner and Leni in *The Trial*, and the Bridge Inn Landlady, Gisa, and Frieda in *The Castle*.

Not only did Kafka see his mother swallowed up in the masculine world of his father but he also lost her to a succession of younger brothers and sisters. Between 1885 when Kafka was two years old and 1892 when he was nine, she gave birth to five children. Two of them died in infancy.

When a young boy feels that he has lost his mother, he is defenseless, particularly in relation to the father. For such a boy, there is no sanctuary. And when the body is frail and the father threatening, the need for sanctuary is all the greater. Kafka had a double vulnerability, a weak body and a lost mother, and together, we believe, they go far in explaining the course that Kafka's life took. We do not deny that Kafka had a father complex but we feel that the severity of this complex can be attributed to a weak body and a lost mother. It is scarcely to be wondered at that he often thought of suicide and why he wrecked himself physically. "The joy again of imagining a knife twisted in my heart" (D1, p. 129). This was not so much an expression of masochism as it was a wish for death.

KAFKA'S FEMININE ORIENTATION

It is now generally accepted by biologists and psychologists that males and females are constitutionally bisexual, and that there is considerable variation within each sex in the relative proportion of masculine and feminine characteristics. In addition to the constitutional determinants, there are environmental influences which act upon and modify the individual's innate predisposition. It is not only difficult to ascertain the relative contributions of constitution and environment but it has also not been possible to reach consensus on what constitutes *psychological* masculinity and femininity.

In attempting to assess the amount of femininity in Kafka's

make-up, we have followed the procedure of comparing the incidence of various dream categories with both male and female norms. It was pointed out in Chapter 2 that Kafka's aggressive and friendly interactions with males and females in his dreams conformed more to a female than to a male pattern. He, like the average female, expressed ambivalence toward both sexes. Moreover, the incidence of aggression and sex deviates from the male norms in the direction of the norms for females. Passivity characterizes his dreams as it seems to have pervaded his waking life.

Two other features of Kafka's dreams resemble the norms for females. One is the high incidence of clothing references. The other lies in the theoretical categories which comprise the three aspects of the castration complex. The incidence of castration wish *plus* the incidence of penis envy is *greater* than the incidence of castration anxiety in female dream series and *smaller* in male dream series (Hall and Van de Castle, 1965). Kafka, like the typical female dreamer, has more castration wish *plus* penis envy than castration anxiety.

In the light of these findings, it appears that Kafka had a feminine orientation although exactly how strong we cannot say. His passivity in waking life has already been noted. Passivity may be due, however, to the inhibition of impulses which prevents the fulfillment of masculine goals, as well as to a feminine temperament or identification. There is little evidence to suggest that Kafka was "effeminate" and much that indicates that many of his interests were masculine. From Brod's description of Kafka, one receives the impression of manliness. It is our impression that his writings are more masculine than feminine although we must confess that we know of no quantitative evidence to support this impression nor do we know of attempts to quantify the differences, if any, between male and female writers except a minor contribution by Hall and Domhoff (1963a) and the suggestive work of McCurdy (see especially 1965, p. 43).

HOMOSEXUALITY

Inevitably, the question of homosexuality arises in connection with passivity and femininity in a male. Did Kafka have overt homosexual relations as well as heterosexual ones? There is no record of any, but then there are not likely to be. He was frank about his heterosexual experiences but that does not mean he would have been equally frank about the manifestations of homoerotic feelings. Given the type of relation he had with his father, he could easily have become homosexual. A domineering, rejecting father often evokes a passive, submissive reaction in his son, which is then transferred to other males and may express itself sexually. Kafka may have been passive but he was not submissive to his father nor apparently to anyone else. On the contrary, he refused to go into his father's business, or to do other things that might have won his father's favor. Submissiveness, fortunately for literature, was not one of Kafka's traits.

Kafka had close male friends but he also had close women friends, among them his youngest sister, Felice Bauer, Milena Jesenská, and Dora Dymant. His feelings toward Max Brod, and possibly toward all men, were frankly expressed in the book they started to write together. While traveling they met a girl to whom Kafka was attracted.

Yet I had another reason for yearning so much after Dora [not Dora Dymant], the girl nearest to me in memory. On this morning Samuel [Brod] fell short of what I needed. He was willing to travel with me as my friend, but that was not much. That meant merely my having a fully clothed man beside me all the days of this journey, whose body I could see only in bathing, without even having the faintest desire for such a spectacle. Samuel, to be sure, would let me lay my head on his breast if I wanted to weep there, but in his presence, at the sight of his masculine face, his neat pointed beard wagging, his tightly shut mouth—I need say no more—could the tears of deliverance ever rise to my eyes at all? (Kafka, 1948, pp. 297–98.)

The psychoanalytically oriented reader will observe the denial in this passage, "without even having the faintest desire" to see Max's body. We know from Kafka's dreams and from his diaries of his interest in nude male bodies which both attracted and repelled him.

There are some indications in his diaries and writings of a homosexual orientation. It will be recalled that his Utopian dream consisted of a community of single men. All of the heroes in Kafka's stories and novels are bachelors. In his diaries, he wrote, "I imagine that I have remained in Paris, walk through it arm in arm with my uncle, pressed close to his side" (D2, p. 79). This uncle, a bachelor, was a favorite of Kafka's. Of a man he meets, he observes, "Happy little B. . . . In this connection it occurs to me—but this is already forced—that toward evening he wanted to come home with me" (D2, p. 218). And of a male lecturer he heard, "I felt that Richepin had an effect upon me such as Solomon must have felt when he took young girls into his bed" (D1, p. 148). In a letter to Milena, he calls himself "the Pawn of the Pawn" and "against all the rules of the game . . . even want to occupy the place of the Queen . . ." (M, p. 73). He also told Milena that she resembled his first male friend. He and Max Brod kissed but that was not unusual probably for the times and the place. Kafka seems to have been genuinely fond of Janouch who was almost half Kafka's age when they became friends. Once Kafka commented on Janouch eying some prostitutes. Janouch replied that the women did not interest him " 'As a matter of fact, I am only interested—in their customers.' Kafka gave me a sidelong glance . . ." (Janouch, 1953, p. 104). Another time, Janouch formed close friendships with three young men. When Kafka expressed his disapproval, Janouch broke off his relationship with them.

The most overt allusion to love between men we could find in Kafka's writings is in *Memoirs of the Kalda Railroad,* "and finally we [two males] fell together on the bunk in an embrace that often lasted ten hours unbroken" (D2, p. 83). Another possible homosexual reference is found in *The Castle* when K. dreams that the secretary who is talking to him turns into a naked Greek god. They fight or "was it a fight at all? This Greek god squeaked like a girl being tickled" (p. 248). In a deleted passage in *The Trial,* Joseph K. carresses and strokes the painter, Titorelli (pp. 308–9).

Goodman (1947) sees a great deal of homosexuality in *The Trial,* and Neider (1962) finds homosexuality in *Amerika.* It is true that there are several episodes in *Amerika,* for example, Karl's visit to the Stoker's cabin and his relations with his uncle and his uncle's friends which suggest homosexuality. It is difficult for us to find convincing evidence of a *great deal* of homosexuality in *The Trial.* It may be remarked here that homosexual interpretations of literature have become faddish in recent years. Whether this trend is due to a greater incidence of homosexual writers, homosexual critics, and homosexual readers, or to some other factor, it is difficult to say.

One of Kafka's dreams (No. 5) has homosexual implications, and in another he is changed into a woman (No. 37).

The foregoing evidence indicates that homoerotic feelings could come to the surface, but considering their relative scarcity they were either not very strong or they were held firmly in check. It is pretty evident that Kafka's heterosexual impulses were restrained, and his homosexual ones may also have been.

What about the theme of the masculinized woman which is

found in Kafka's dreams and in his writings? We see no necessary relationship between it and homosexuality. We have already suggested that this conception of women stemmed from his mother whom he saw as his father's ally. It caused Kafka to be suspicious and distrustful of women but it did not turn him to seek out homosexual relations with men.

Our final conclusion is that Kafka was not effeminate and that overt sexual relations with males were not an outlet for him. He may very well have had latent homosexual impulses that occasionally expressed themselves in displaced or symbolic ways, but this would not distinguish Kafka from the bulk of mankind. Nor do we feel that the evidence suggests there were strong conflicts over homosexuality in his personal life or that his writings are heavily impregnated with homoerotic themes, disguised or otherwise.

THE DECEASED BROTHERS

Hermann and Julie Kafka had six children within a period of ten years. The order of their births and the years they died are as follows:

> Franz Kafka, 1883–1924
> George Kafka, 1885–87
> Heinrich Kafka, 1887–88
> Gabriele Kafka, 1889–1944?
> Valerie Kafka, 1890–1944?
> Ottilie Kafka, 1892–1944?

Kafka was the first child, born the year following his parents' marriage. When Kafka was two years old, a brother was born. George lived less than two years. In the same year that he died a second brother was born and he died the next year. Thus, during the first five years of Kafka's life two brothers were born and died.

(Kafka's three sisters were believed to have been murdered in Auschwitz in 1944.)

If the psychoanalytic view that children typically harbor death wishes against younger siblings is accepted, the actual death of two brothers should have been very traumatic for the surviving older brother. We have already noted the presence of pairs of characters or objects in Kafka's writings. K. treats his two assistants so badly that they almost die. The two assistants in the short story *Blumfeld* are a great trial to their boss. Two wardens arrest Joseph K. and two men kill him. Two vagabonds in *Amerika* get Karl into a lot of trouble.

Although there is no direct evidence of the possible influence of these sibling deaths on Kafka's personality, at the very least they must have made it all the harder for Kafka to deal with a rejecting father and mother. If he held himself responsible for their deaths—and young children are supposed to believe in the omnipotence of their wishes—then young Franz would have one more reason for feeling unworthy of being loved.

In Paul Goodman's (1947) chaotic but richly allusive book, *Kafka's Prayer*, he writes: "I would hazard the guess that Kafka's lifelong duel with his father, that looms so large in the foreground, is partly a covering device for a deeper trouble, a savage and irreparable destruction perhaps committed by himself, that is only hinted at" (p. 85). We share the same view. However, we do not agree with Goodman when later (p. 112) he suggests that it was the death of the two brothers that was "the deeper trouble." We still believe that the main decisive factors in determining the course of Kafka's life were his own frail body and the loss of his mother.

CASTRATION ANXIETY

Fear of losing the mother's love and fear of castration by the father are the two great fears of childhood according to Freud. Their traumatic effects and how the child defends against them profoundly influence personality and behavior throughout life.

We have seen that there are no elements in any of Kafka's dreams that could be scored as indicative of castration anxiety according to the criteria we followed. This is rather surprising in view of his fear of his father, his aversion to his body, and the disfigurement theme in his dreams. We propose the hypothesis that Kafka did not express castration anxiety in his dreams because he already felt castrated. There was nothing any longer to fear from that side.

For a man who feels castrated several options are available. He can, for example, assume the feminine role as passive homosexuals do. That Kafka was passive is evident, but we rejected the notion that he was overtly homosexual. Had he been able to identify with his mother and had he been willing to submit to the authority of his father, he might have become an overt homosexual. He could not identify with his mother because he saw her as being in league with his father, nor could he submit to his father because of some hard core of stubbornness in his make-up. Unlike Georg in *The Judgment* who committed suicide at his father's bidding, Kafka actually fought his father at every turn. When Kafka fell in love it was with a forceful woman like his mother as well as like his father who was a very dominant man. But he could not consummate these love affairs in marriage because he refused to give up his freedom to write. Writing for Kafka was the rock on which his whole life was founded, and anything that threatened to dispossess him of this rock was cast off. Writing gave Kafka a reason for living. It alone, we believe, compensated for his feeling of being castrated.

A man who feels castrated is not likely to enjoy sexual relations with women because they, having suffered the same fate that he has, are a constant reminder of his defect. Kafka seems not to have had a very active sex life in spite of his attractiveness to women. His dreams indicate that he considered women to be disfigured and he had a similar aversion to their bodies as he had for his own. In a letter to Milena (M, p. 171) he wrote, "I like to hold your hand in mine, I like to look into your eyes. That's about all."

His preoccupation with clothes can be understood as a need to conceal the naked body. It is possible also that Kafka's interest in men's clothes was a defense against jealousy or temptation or both. Yet he was drawn to a nudist colony, spent considerable time at swimming baths, and dreamed about nakedness. It is a reasonable assumption that Kafka secretly liked to look at male bodies although professing to be repelled by them. Possibly he indulged in sado-masochistic fantasies. Such a fantasy, in fact, appears in the chapter, "The Whipper" in *The Trial*. Joseph K. happens to look into a storage room at his place of work and sees the following scene. There are three men, one of whom is about to whip the other two. The whipper "was sheathed in a sort of dark leather garment which left his throat and a good deal of his chest and the whole of his arms bare" (p. 104). He "was tanned like a sailor and had a brutal, healthy face" (p. 106). The victims were instructed to take off all their clothes so they could be flogged. In *The Penal Colony* is another vivid sado-masochistic fantasy, as is Dream 25.

Our thesis is that castration held no threat for Kafka because he had already accepted it as a *fait accompli*. Unable to submit either to a dominant female, which he tried to do without success, or to a dominant male which he probably never tried (Brod did not fill the bill), he found in writing a compensation for his castrated condition. The pen became a substitute for the lost penis. It became the tool of generativity. By means of it, he overcame father and mother, brawny men and forceful women, and his own passivity. By his pen, he fathered the works that were to make him immortal.

THE PROBLEM OF GUILT

The absence of guilt in Kafka's dreams may come as a surprise to those who see in Kafka's writings, especially *The Trial*, a profound, existential concern with man's guilt. Hubben (1962), to name but one of many critics, avers that Kafka's major theme "is an ever present sense of guilt" (p. 143). When we examine *The Trial*, however, we see that Joseph K., despite his arrest, does not feel guilty. Rather he bends every effort to learn what the crime is that he is charged with so that he can defend himself. At the end of the book, when an official plunges a knife into Joseph K's heart, he feels ashamed to be dying like a dog. He is humiliated but not guilty.

It may be objected that although Joseph K. may not have felt guilty, nevertheless *The Trial* is about a man who is guilty of a crime; otherwise why should he have been arrested? Guilt, as defined by society, and a sense of guilt may be two quite different things, however. Some people convicted of the most horrendous crimes never feel guilty, whereas some innocent people suffer enormous guilt feelings. Freud observed many years ago that a good man often feels guiltier than a bad man.

The "boundless sense of guilt" that Kafka confessed to did not arise solely from his own conduct but was largely associated with the actions of his father.

"I had lost my self-confidence where you were concerned, and in its place had developed a boundless sense of guilt. (In recollection of this boundlessness I once wrote of someone, accurately: 'He is afraid the shame will outlive him, even.') I could not suddenly change when I was with other people; rather, I came to feel an even deeper sense of guilt with them, for, as I have already said, I had to make up to them for the wrongs you had done them in your business, wrongs in which I too had my share of the responsibility" (LF, p. 73). Even in this passage, Kafka refers to the shame that "will outlive him [Joseph K.]," thereby confusing shame with guilt. The two are not synonymous.

Feelings of shame ordinarily result from a personal inadequacy in dealing appropriately with a situation. Shame varies in degree from a slight embarrassment to an abject humiliation. Feelings of guilt arise from having done something or thought something contrary to one's moral or ethical standards. In Freudian terminology, shame is evoked by an inadequacy of the ego whereas guilt results from a transgression of the superego. Joseph K. felt ashamed to be dying like a dog but he did not feel guilty. Kafka felt ashamed of his father but he did not feel guilty. He also felt ashamed of his body.

Kafka's diaries do not contain confessions of guilt, nor do his letters to Milena. Brod does not mention that Kafka was weighed down by a sense of guilt. In the light of all this evidence, it is questionable whether Kafka was unduly plagued by guilt feelings.

Guilt feelings are not, however, always expressed directly but may be revealed in indirect ways. A favorite device in dreams is for the dreamer to be punished or threatened by an authority figure, e.g., a policeman, or to suffer a misfortune such as an accident or an injury. In such cases, it is assumed that the dreamer's conscience is punishing him for a violation of his moral code. One of us (Hall, 1966a) has discussed this conflict between impulse (id) and conscience (superego) at some length.

We have already seen, however, that the number of misfortunes Kafka experiences in his dreams does not deviate significantly from the norms. Nor is he the victim of an authority figure. A policeman comes into only one dream (No. 19) and plays a helpful rather than a threatening role.

Politzer (1962) says that "Kafka's vision of punishment ultimately grew out of his own guilt feelings" (p. 163), and this view is supported by Dream 30 in which Kafka welcomes the punishment that resulted from his being implicated in a crime. But this is the only dream of this sort and does not distinguish Kafka from other dreamers. It merely shows that Kafka had a conscience as virtually all men have. Politzer's interpretation is not invalidated thereby since the need for punishment probably always grows out of guilt feelings. Kafka, it may be assumed, used the human condition which he discovered in himself for literary purposes. Kafka was not, however, a guilt-ridden person. His guilt complex was no stronger than that of other men.

In this chapter, we have used information obtained from a content analysis of Kafka's dreams for the purpose of identifying some of the crucial conditions that shaped Kafka's personality and behavior. The two determinants that seemed to have played a decisive role were Kafka's aversion to his body and the feeling that his mother had deserted him. With the identification of these two factors, Kafka's behavior in his dreams as well as in waking life—his passivity, his ambivalence toward women, his scoptophilia, his preoccupation with body disfigurement, his mixed feelings about his father, to name only a few—become more understandable. This formulation also helps to explicate the themes about which he wrote.

6. REALIZATIONS

Modern dream theories stress the compensatory or wishfulfilling function of dreams. Dreams are supposed to correct the imbalances in one's personality, to overcome the frustrations, and to resolve the conflicts that plague one's life. Dreaming has been likened to a safety valve by which the accumulated tensions of the day are discharged so that we awaken refreshed in mind as well as in body. Dreaming has also been viewed as a homeostatic process that helps to maintain one's mental equilibrium. Dreams, according to these theories, are discontinuous with waking life. They tell us, in effect, that we *are* in our dreams what we *are not* when awake.

This study of Kafka's dreams in relation to his life indicates that dreams are more likely to be continuous with waking life. According to a simple wish-fulfillment hypothesis, Kafka who was clearly discontented with his body should have dreamed about having a better physique. In one dream (No. 22), it is true, he does acquire a large sword which may be interpreted as compensation for a felt lack of virility, but body disfigurement and passivity are much more characteristic of Kafka's dreams. We found that what occupied Kafka's thoughts and how he behaved during the day were what he dreamed about during the night. The principle of congruence or continuity fits the data better than the principle of compensation or discontinuity.

This investigation has generated other information about the uses of the content analysis of dreams for understanding personality. For example, the analysis of Kafka's dreams revealed complexes and conflicts that could not be readily identified from biographical or autobiographical material. The conception of the masculine woman does not express itself directly in biography or diaries,[1] yet having found it in his dreams it helps us to under-

1. There is a reference to a "male impersonator" in his *Diaries* (D1, pp. 79, 86). This was an actress who was dressed as a man.

stand why his relations with his mother and with other women were so ambivalent. Similarly, the scoptophilic theme in his dreams sheds light upon many features of his waking behavior.

The content analysis of dreams can also serve a valuable function by pointing to aspects of behavior that otherwise might be overlooked. Questions may be raised which lead one to search for new information about the person. For example, the question of whether Kafka was overtly homosexual was raised and although it could not be decisively answered for want of information, future scholarship may be able to answer it. In Kafka's case, this function of dream analysis is not so important since he was a very introspective person and recorded many of his innermost thoughts. It would be hard not to notice the concern with his body or with clothes from reading his diaries, but disfigurement and the masculine woman might remain unnoticed were it not for the dreams. Moreover, since Kafka was a writer it was possible for us to correlate material in his dreams with a content analysis of his writings, thereby enhancing or facilitating our understanding of them.

An example of how dreams may bring to light unusual features in an author's writings is furnished by the American-French novelist, Julian Green. Green (1939) observes, "In all my books, the conception of fear or of any other of the stronger forms of emotion seems in some unaccountable way to be connected with a staircase." After giving instances from his novels, he says, "When I was a child I used to dream that I was being pursued on a staircase." He also reports a nightmare he had when he was an adult involving a person descending a staircase.

In addition to elucidating and directing attention to personal and behavioral manifestations, dreams also enable one to locate a common factor or motive underlying diverse forms of behavior. The identification of scoptophilia in Kafka's dreams helps to explain his interest in the theater, nudism, walking, swimming, travel, reading preferences, and his vocation as a writer. Phenotypic (behavioral) diversity is thereby reduced to genotypic (motivational) unity. Dreams reveal what these basic motives are probably better than any other type of material. We can begin to make sense out of the pluralism of waking behavior by observing coherent patterns of repeated themes in dreams.

Inevitably, the analysis of dreams raises questions concerning the origins of behavior. Dreams, we believe, are, in part, a reflection of the timeless unconscious; timeless because the wishes and fears of early childhood continue to express themselves in one's dreams throughout life. This is brought out in a study made by Smith and Hall (1964). We believe that the infantile wishes and fears in the timeless unconscious furnish the main motive forces for adult behavior. In Kafka's case, his feelings about his body and about his mother which appeared in early childhood were the main determinants of his adult character and behavior. Rejection by the mother meant that he could not cope with the father nor could he establish a satisfying and permanent relationship with a woman. Rejection of his body resulted in neurasthenia and hypochondria and was one of the reasons for his becoming consumptive.

Although dreams bear a direct relationship to waking life, there are complexities in the nature of the relationship. One complexity results from the different idioms employed in dreams and in behavior. Both idioms are the metaphorical acting out of wishes and fears in the timeless unconscious, but the acting out in dreams is not bound by the same regard for physical and social realities that govern to some extent the acting out of wishes and fears in waking life. Kafka's dream of his and Milena's bodies merging in flames could scarcely have happened in waking life, yet his feelings for her were accurately symbolized in the dream.

In waking life, he expressed these feelings in a different idiom. Another example is the dream in which Kafka prevents his father from falling out of the window by holding on to the loops of his bathrobe. Implausible as this imagery may be, nevertheless it portrays with the utmost clarity and accuracy Kafka's unbreakable tie to his father.

When it is said that there is a continuity between dreams and life, we do not mean that the actions and interactions of life are carried over intact into dreams, although sometimes they may be. We mean that the significance of dreams and the significance of behavior are the same. Different symbols for the same referent may be used in dreams and in waking life, in which case the symbols are *dynamically equivalent* although in outward form dissimilar. The nature of the referent is often more easily discovered by analyzing dreams than by analyzing waking behavior.

The analysis of the symbolism of our behavior and of those everyday objects with which we interact can be done without resorting to dreams but it requires putting to one side our reasonable, common-sense orientation which attributes logic, utility, or habit to everything we do, except that which is plainly aberrant. If we were to regard our daily existence as a continuous and repetitious metaphorical acting out of conflicts and complexes laid down in childhood, we would begin to understand the significance of our behavior in the same way that we try to understand the significance of our dreams. It is just because so many dreams are "unrealistic," and the same is true of bizarre waking behavior, that we are willing to forego common-sense explanations of them.

It is by means of studies such as this one in which Kafka's dreams and waking behavior were reduced to a common set of themes that the continuity of dreams and waking life will be established, and we can begin to develop a broad and useful science of personality. By dissociating dreams from life, we forfeit some of our best data for understanding the nature of man and the world he has created (Hall, 1962).

This study has also demonstrated the value of an objective, quantitative methodology for analyzing dreams and literature. The results obtained by employing such a methodology possess the virtues of replicability, the application of tests of statistical significance, and comparability with other similar investigations and with norms. The analysis of verbal material such as dream reports and stories becomes a scientific enterprise when a quantitative methodology is used. With the aid of computers, the investigator can extend the scope of his analysis immeasurably. The formulation and specification of appropriate categories for making a content analysis of verbal material is the most crucial feature of the methodology. The most appropriate categories, in our opinion, are those which emerge out of and fairly represent the empirical structure of the verbal material. Such categories tell what is actually there and with what frequency, thereby providing a firm empirical basis for inference and theorizing. Theoretical categories when they are formulated with due regard for the theory from which they are derived are also useful, especially for testing specific hypotheses regarding personality. (For a fuller discussion of categories see Hall, 1969a, 1969b.)

Let us conclude by saying something about the man who made this study possible. Contrary to the saying "Familiarity breeds contempt," our admiration for Kafka's remarkably disciplined creativity and for the esthetic, moral, and psychological values of his writings steadily grew throughout the period of our engagement with him. Much has been written about the "terror of art" in connection with Kafka. We feel this is a grave error of interpretation. Art, for Kafka, was not the refuge or the wrack of a terrorized or terrified man. It was a continual exercise in self-understanding and self-expression. Kafka's demons were purged not on the psychoanalytic couch but by the relentless, clear-eyed explorations of the "nethermost" limits of his being. The legacies of these explorations—the diaries, the letters, the parables, the meditations, the stories, and the novels—is unsurpassed in modern literature. Anyone who does not emerge from a reading of Kafka with a clearer view of the inexhaustible ironies and paradoxes of the human condition—a human condition that is bound to no definite place or time—has not really read him.

As for the man, it seems to us, Urzidil (1968) captured in words what must have been the "magic" of his "presence." Writing of the effect of Kafka's entrance into a meeting room, Urzidil says, "It seemed . . . as though some unseen attendant had whispered to the lecturer: 'Be careful about everything you say from now on. For Kafka has just arrived.' This irresistible magic always represented to me evidence of the eternal. And it is still viable today. Never before have I had the definite feeling in the presence of any other genius whom I had the good fortune and honor to meet, of the sudden change in the inner coordinating system of an entire audience or group, indeed even of the actual spatial proportions of an assembly room resulting from the mere silent presence of a personality" (pp. 102–3). Fortunately, for our generation and for all future ones, the magic of Kafka's presence shines through everything he wrote.

Franz Kafka was born in Prague, July 3, 1883, and died of tuberculosis in a sanatorium near Vienna, June 3, 1924. He was the
eldest of six children born to Hermann and Julie (Löwy) Kafka
who were married in 1882. Two sons died in infancy and three
daughters born in 1889, 1890, and 1892, respectively, were
murdered by the Nazis in 1944. Both parents outlived Franz. His
father died in 1932 at the age of 79, his mother in 1934 at the age
of 78.

Hermann Kafka, the son of a butcher, was a strong, energetic,
and domineering man who established a successful wholesale
haberdashery warehouse in Prague. The family lived in comfort-
able circumstances. Franz's mother's family, according to Brod,
consisted of "scholars, dreamers inclined to eccentricity, and
others driven by this inclination to the adventurous, the exotic,
or the freakish and reclusive" (B, p. 6). Mrs. Kafka seems not to
have displayed any of these traits, however. She helped her husband in his business, had a number of children in quick succession, and maintained a middle-class home.

Franz was raised as a German and a Jew. He attended German
schools and the German University in Prague. Later in his life,
Kafka acquired a thorough knowledge of the Czech language and
its literature, but all of his writing was done in German.

Kafka began his studies at the university in 1901 and earned a
doctorate in law in 1906. He worked in various capacities as a
lawyer for two years before accepting a position with the Workers' Accident Insurance Institute in Prague. He held the same
position until illness forced his retirement near the end of his
life. The principal advantages of this job were its security and
the hours of work. Kafka was usually through at the office by
early afternoon so that he had the rest of the day for writing and
other intellectual and cultural pursuits. Kafka began to write
while he was a university student, and was first published in 1909.
But it was not until 1912 at the age of twenty-nine, according to
Politzer (1962), that he made his literary breakthrough and discovered a style of writing that was uniquely his own. This first

Kafkaesque story, *The Judgment,* was written in a burst of creative inspiration during one sitting. Thereafter, Kafka was continuously engaged in literary activity although few of his works were published during his lifetime. This failure to be published was not for want of a publisher but was due solely to Kafka's own reluctance to have his writings appear in print. Indeed, he instructed Brod to destroy his manuscripts upon Kafka's death.

It was also in 1912 that Kafka met Felice Bauer, a Berlin woman, who was to play such a large part in his life for the next five years. Twice engaged, this ambivalent relationship was finally terminated in 1917 when Kafka discovered he had tuberculosis. In 1919, he was engaged briefly to a girl he met at a summer resort, and in 1920 he met and fell in love with Milena Jesenská, a married woman living in Vienna with her husband. For two years, they wrote fervid and frequent letters to each other but they had few meetings. In the last year of his life, he lived with and was cared for by a young German girl, Dora Dymant. Kafka is believed to have fathered a child during a brief affair with a woman around 1913.

Kafka lived in his parents' home throughout his life except for brief periods when he occupied bachelor quarters in Prague, visited his sister in the country, or was a patient in various sanatoria.

Kafka's genius as a writer and his immense influence on twentieth-century thought are now recognized throughout the world.

NOTE: While this was being written (August, 1968) Russian troops invaded Czechoslovakia to put down a liberal movement there. Stephen Spender writing in the *New York Review of Books* (August 22, 1968) observes that this "liberalizing movement among the writers and teachers began with a conference on [Kafka's] writings held by the members of the Academy of Learning in 1963. . . . The conference led to the rehabilitation of Kafka and to a general attack on censorship."

In presenting these dreams we necessarily had to take them out of the context of the diaries and letters in which they appeared, and thus out of the context of Kafka's life. In order to rectify this, we have included some information about what Kafka was doing about the time he reported each dream. In cases where the dreams occurred relatively close together, we have given biographical information for groups of dreams rather than to repeat the same information for each dream. The purpose of including this material is only to place the dream within Kafka's life at the time and not to imply any causal relationship or interpretation. Kafka's own comments on his dreams are enclosed by brackets, and the biographical notes are enclosed by parentheses.

Dream 1. May, 1910, c. Age 26, Diaries 1, *pp. 9–10.*

In a dream I asked the dancer Eduardova to dance the Czardas just one time more. She had a broad streak of shadow or light across the middle of her face between the lower part of her forehead and the cleft of her chin. Just then someone with the loathsome gestures of an unconscious intriguer approached to tell her the train was leaving immediately. The manner in which she listened to this announcement made it terribly clear to me that she would not dance again. "I am a wicked, evil woman, am I not?" she said. "Oh no," I said, "not that," and turned away aimlessly.

Before that I had questioned her about the many flowers that were stuck into her girdle. "They are from all the princes of Europe," said she. I pondered as to what this might mean—that all those fresh flowers stuck in her girdle had been presented to the dancer Eduardova by all the princes of Europe.

(On May 4, 1910, Kafka and Brod went to see a theatrical performance which was the beginning for Kafka of a long association with this Yiddish troupe. Eduardova was not a member of this troupe. Kafka "fell in love" with one of the actresses and also became intensely interested in one of the actors, Isak Lowy. Kafka began to write a "kind of autobiography" of Lowy along with a survey of the Yiddish theater which characteristically was never completed. Kafka also actively solicited engagements for the troupe and sometimes traveled with them. Kafka's interest in the performers and the theater is clearly evident in some of his later dreams, Nos. 7, 8, and 10.)

Dream 2. October 2, 1911, Age 28, Diaries 1, pp. 74–75.

The horrible apparition last night of a blind child, apparently the daughter of my aunt in Leitmeritz who, however, has no daughter but only sons, one of whom once broke his leg. On the other hand there were resemblances between this child and Dr. M.'s daughter who, as I have recently seen, is in the process of changing from a pretty child into a stout, stiffly dressed little girl. This blind or weak-sighted child had both eyes covered by a pair of eyeglasses, the left, under a lens held at a certain distance from the eyes was milky-gray and bulbous, the other receded and was covered by a lens lying close against it. In order that this eyeglass might be set in place with optical correctness it was necessary, instead of the usual support going back of the ears, to make use of a lever, the head of which could be attached no place but to the cheekbone, so that from this lens a little rod descended to the cheek, there disappeared into the pierced flesh and ended on the bone, while another small wire rod came out and went back over the ear.

[I was so weak today that I even told my chief the story of the child. I remembered that the eyeglasses in the dream derive from my mother, who in the evening sits next to me and while playing cards looks across at me not very pleasantly under her eyeglasses. Her eyeglasses even have, which I do not remember having noticed before, the right lens nearer the eye than the left.]

(Dreams 2–10. During the months of August and September, 1911, Kafka and Brod took a trip to Switzerland, Italy, and Paris. After this trip Kafka went to the Erlenbach health resort in Switzerland.)

Dream 3. October 9, 1911, Age 28, Diaries 1, *pp. 88–90.*

I walked—whether Max was there right at the start I don't know—through a long row of houses at the level of the first or second floor, just as one walks through a tunnel from one carriage to another. I walked very quickly, perhaps also because the house was so rickety that for that reason alone one hurried. The doors between the houses I did not notice at all, it was just a gigantic row of rooms, and yet not only the differences between the individual apartments but also between the houses were recognizable. They were perhaps all rooms with beds through which I went. One typical bed has remained in my memory. It stood at the side to the left of me against the dark or dirty wall, which sloped like an attic's, perhaps had a low pile of bedclothes, and its cover, really only a coarse sheet crumpled by the feet of the person who had slept here, hung down in a point. I felt abashed to walk through people's rooms at a time when many of them were still lying in their beds, therefore took long strides on tiptoes, by which I somehow or other hoped to show that I was passing through only by compulsion, was as considerate of everything as was at all possible, walked softly, and that my passing through did not, as it were, count at all. Therefore, too, I never turned my head in any one room and saw only either what lay on the right toward the street or on the left toward the back wall.

The row of houses was often interrupted by brothels; and although I was making this journey seemingly because of them, I walked through them especially quickly so that I remember nothing except that they were there. However, the last room of all the houses was again a brothel, and here I remained. The wall across from the door through which I entered, therefore the last wall of the row of houses, was either of glass or merely broken through, and if I had walked on I should have fallen. It is even more probable that it was broken through, for the whores lay toward the edge of the floor. Two I saw clearly on the ground, the head of one hung down a little over the edge into the open air. To the left was a solid wall, on the other hand the wall on the right was not finished, you could see down into the court, even if not to the bottom of it, and a ramshackle gray staircase led down in several flights. To judge by the light in the room the ceiling was like that in the other rooms.

I occupied myself chiefly with the whore whose head was hanging down, Max with one lying beside her on the left. I fingered her legs and then for a long time pressed the upper parts of her thighs in regular rhythm. My pleasure in this was so great that I wondered that for this entertainment which was after all really the most beautiful kind, one still had to pay nothing. I was convinced that I (and I alone) deceived the world. Then the whore, without moving her legs, raised the upper part of her body and turned her back to me, which to my horror was covered with large scaling-wax-red circles with paling edges, and red splashes scattered among them. I now noticed that her whole body was full of them, that I was pressing my thumb to her thighs in just such spots and that there were these little red particles—as though from a crumbled seal—on my fingers too.

I stepped back among a number of men who seemed to be waiting against the wall near the opening of the stairway, on which there was a small amount of traffic. They were waiting in the way men in the country stand together in the market place on Sunday morning. Therefore it was Sunday too. It was here that the comic scene took place, when a man I and Max had reason to be afraid of went away, then came up the stairs, then stepped up to me, and while I and Max anxiously expected some terrible threat from him, put a ridiculously simple-minded question to me. Then I stood there and with apprehension watched Max, who, without fear in this place, was sitting on the ground somewhere to the left eating a thick potato soup out of which the potatoes peeped like large balls, especially one. He pushed them down into the soup with his spoon, perhaps with two spoons, or just turned them.

(Kafka mentions visiting brothels on his journey with Brod.)

Dream 4. October 28, 1911, Age 28, Diaries 1, p. 119.

I dreamed today of a donkey that looked like a greyhound, it was very cautious in its movements. I looked at it closely because

I was aware how unusual a phenomenon it was, but remember only that its narrow human feet could not please me because of their length and uniformity. I offered it a bunch of fresh, dark-green cypress leaves which I had just received from an old Zurich lady (it all took place in Zurich), it did not want it, just sniffed a little at it; but then, when I left the cypress on a table, it devoured it so completely that only a scarcely recognizable kernel resembling a chestnut was left. Later there was talk that this donkey had never yet gone on all fours but always held itself erect like a human being and showed its silvery shining breast and its little belly. But actually that was not correct.

Dream 5. October 28, 1911, Age 28, Diaries 1, pp. 119–20.

Besides this, I dreamed about an Englishman whom I met at a meeting like the one the Salvation Army held in Zurich. There were seats there like those in school, under the blackboard there was even an open shelf; once when I reached in to straighten something I wondered at the ease with which one makes friends on a trip. By this apparently was meant the Englishman, who shortly thereafter approached me. He had loose, light clothes in very good condition, but high up on the back of the arms, instead of the material of the clothing, or at least sewn on over it, there was a gray, wrinkled material, hanging a little, torn in strips, stippled as though by spiders, that reminded one as much of the leather re-enforcements on riding breeches as of the sleeve protectors of seamstresses, salesgirls, clerks. His face was also covered with a gray material that had very clever slits for mouth, eyes, probably also for the nose. But this material was new, napped, rather like flannel, very flexible and soft, of excellent English manufacture. All this pleased me so, that I was eager to become acquainted with the man. He wanted to invite me to his house too, but since I had to leave as soon as the day after tomorrow, that came to nothing. Before he left the meeting he put on several more apparently very practical pieces of clothing that made him look quite inconspicuous after he had buttoned them. Although he could not invite me to his home, he nevertheless asked me to go into the street with him. I followed him, we stopped across the street from the meeting place on the curb, I below, he above, and found again after some discussion that nothing could be done about the invitation.

Dream 6. October 28, 1911, Age 28, Diaries 1, p. 120.

Then I dreamed that Max, Otto and I had the habit of packing our trunks only when we reached the railroad station. There we were, carrying our shirts, for example, through the main hall to our distant trunks. Although this seemed to be a general custom, it was not a good one in our case, especially since we have begun to pack only shortly before the arrival of the train. Then we were naturally excited and had hardly any hope of still catching the train, let alone getting good seats.

Dream 7. November 9, 1911, Age 28, Diaries 1, pp. 142–44.

Everything theater, I now up in the balcony, now on the stage, a girl whom I had liked a few months ago was playing a part, tensed her lithe body when she held on to the back of a chair in terror; from the balcony I pointed to the girl who was playing a male role, my companion did not like her. In one act the set was so large that nothing else was to be seen, no stage, no auditorium, no dark, no footlights; instead, great crowds of spectators were on the set which represented the Altstadter Ring, probably seen from the opening of Niklasstrasse. Although one should really not have been able to see the square in front of the Rathaus clock and the small Ring, short turns and slow rockings of the stage floor nevertheless made it possible to look down, for example, on the small Ring from Kinsky Palace. This had no purpose except to show the whole set whenever possible, since it was already there in such perfection anyhow, and since it would have been a crying shame to miss seeing any of this set which, as I was well aware, was the most beautiful set in all the world and of all time. The lighting was that of dark, autumnal clouds. The light of the dimmed sun was scatteredly reflected from one or another stained-glass window on the southeast side of the square. Since everything was executed in life size and without the smallest false detail, the fact that some of the casement windows were blown open and shut by the slight breeze without a sound because of the great height of the houses, made an overwhelming impression. The square was very steep, the pavement almost black, the Tein Church was in its place, but in front of it was a small imperial castle in the courtyard of which all the monuments that ordinarily stood in the square were assembled in perfect order: the Pillar of St. Mary, the old fountain in front of the Rathaus that I myself have never seen, the fountain before the Niklas Church, and a board fence that has now been put up around the excavation for the Hus memorial.

They acted—in the audience one often forgets that it is only acting, how much truer is this on the stage and behind the scenes—an imperial fete and a revolution. The revolution, with huge throngs of people sent back and forth, was probably greater than anything that ever took place in Prague; they had apparently located it in Prague only because of the set, although really it belonged in Paris. Of the fete one saw nothing at first, in any event, the court had ridden off to a fete, meanwhile the revolution had broken out, the people had forced its way into the castle, I myself ran out into the open night over the ledges of the fountain in the churchyard, but it was supposed to be impossible for the court to return to the castle. Then the court carriages came from Eisengasse at so wild a pace that they had to brake while still far from the castle entrance, and slid across the pavement with locked wheels. They were the sort of carriages—one sees them at festivals and processions—on which living tableaux are shown, they were therefore flat, hung with garlands of flowers, and from the carriage floors a colored cloth covering the wheels hung down all around. One was all the more aware of the terror that their speed indicated. As though unconsciously, the horses, which reared before the entrance, pulled the carriages in a curve from Eisengasse to the castle. Just then many people streamed past me out into the square, mostly spectators whom I knew from the street and who perhaps had arrived this very moment. Among them there was also a girl I know, but I do not know which; beside her walked a young, elegant man in a yellowish-brown ulster with small checks, his right hand deep in his pocket. They walked toward Niklasstrasse. From this moment on I saw nothing more.

(Kafka was with his actor friends the day of this dream. He lived on the Altstadter Ring at the time.)

Dream 8. November 19, 1911, Age 28, Diaries 1, pp. 153–56.

In the theater. Performance of Das Weite Land by Schnitzler, adapted by Utitz. I sit all the way up front, think I am sitting in the first row until it finally appears that it is the second. The back of the row is turned toward the stage so that one can see the auditorium comfortably, the stage only by turning. The author is somewhere nearby, I can't hold back my poor opinion of the play which I seem to know from before, but add that the third act is supposed to be witty. With this "supposed to be," however, I mean to say that if one is speaking of the good parts, I do not know the play and must rely on hearsay; therefore I repeat this remark once more, not just for myself, but nevertheless it is disregarded by the others. There is a great crush around me. The audience seems to have come in its winter clothes, everyone fills his seat to overflowing. People beside me, behind me, whom I do not see, interrupt me, point out new arrivals, mention their names, my attention is called especially to a married couple forcing their way along a row of seats, since the woman has a dark-yellow, mannish, longnosed face and besides, as far as one can see in the crowd out of which her head towers, is wearing men's clothes; near me, remarkably free, the actor Lowy, but very unlike the real one, is standing and making excited speeches in which the word "principium" is repeated, I keep expecting the words "tertium comparationis," they do not come. In a box in the second tier, really only in a right-hand corner (seen from the stage) of the balcony that connects with the boxes there, a third son of the Kisch family, dressed in a beautiful Prince Albert with its flaps opened wide, stands behind his mother, who is seated, and speaks out into the theater. Lowy's speeches have a connection with these speeches. Among other things, Kisch points high up to a spot on the curtain and says, There sits the German Kisch, by this he means my schoolmate who studied Germanics. When the curtain goes up the theater begins to darken, and Kisch, in order to indicate that he would disappear in any case, marches up and away from the balcony with his mother, again with all his arms, coats and legs spread wide.

The stage is somewhat lower than the auditorium, you look down with your chin on the back of the seat. The set consists chiefly of two low, thick pillars in the middle of the stage. The scene is a banquet in which girls and young men take part. Despite the fact that when the play began many people in the first rows left, apparently to go backstage, I can see very little, for the girls left behind block the view with their large, flat hats, most of which are blue, that move back and forth along the whole length of the row. Nevertheless, I see a small ten-to-fifteen-year-old boy unusually clearly on the stage. He has dry, parted, straight-cut hair. He cannot even place his napkin properly on his lap, must look down carefully when he does, and is supposed to be a man-about-town in this play. In consequence, I no longer have much confidence in this theater. The company on the stage now waits for various newcomers who come down onto the stage from the first rows of the auditorium. But the play is not well rehearsed, either. Thus, an actress named Hackelberg has just entered, an actor, leaning back in his chair like a man of the world, addresses her as "Hackel," then becomes aware of his mistake and corrects himself. Now a girl enters whom I know (her name is Frankel, I think), she climbs over the back of the seat right where I am sitting, her back, when she climbs over, is entirely naked, the skin not very good, over the right hip there is even a scratched, bloodshot spot the size of a doorknob. But then, when she turns around on the stage and stands there with a clean face, she acts very well. Now a singing horseman is supposed to approach out of the distance at a gallop, a piano reproduces the clatter of hoofs, you hear the stormy song approaching, finally I see the singer too, who, to give the singing the natural swelling that takes place in a rapid approach, is running along the balcony up above toward the stage. He is not yet at the stage or through with the song and yet he has already passed the climax of haste and shrieking song, and the piano too can no longer reproduce distinctly the sound of hoofs striking against the stones. Both stop, therefore, and the singer approaches quietly, but he makes himself so small that only his head rises above the railing of the balcony, so that you cannot see him very clearly.

With this, the first act is over, but the curtain doesn't come down, the theater remains dark too. On the stage two critics sit on the floor, writing, with their backs resting against a piece of scenery. A dramatic coach or stage manager with a blond, pointed beard jumps onto the stage, while still in the air he stretches one hand out to give some instructions, in the other hand he has a bunch of grapes that had been in a fruit dish on the banquet table and which he now eats.

Again facing the auditorium I see that it is lit by simple petroleum lanterns that are stuck up on simple chandeliers, like those in the streets, and now, of course, burn only very low. Suddenly, impure petroleum or a damaged wick is probably the cause, the light spurts out of one of these lanterns and sparks pour down in a broad gush on the crowded audience that forms a mass as black as earth. Then a gentleman rises up out of this mass, walks on it toward the lantern, apparently wants to fix the lantern, but first looks up at it, remains standing near it for a short while and, when nothing happens, returns quietly to his place in which he is swallowed up. I take him for myself and bow my face into the darkness.

(The mannish woman may be the "male impersonator" referred to by Kafka in his diary, D1, p. 79).

Dream 9. November 20, 1911, Age 28, Diaries 1, p. 157.

Dream of a picture, apparently by Ingres. The girls in the woods in a thousand mirrors, or rather: the virgins, etc. To the right of the picture, grouped in the same way and airily drawn like the pictures on theater curtains, there was a more compact group, to the left they sat and lay on a gigantic twig or flying ribbon, or soared by their own power in a chain that rose slowly toward the sky. And now they were reflected not only toward the spectator but also away from him, became more indistinct and multitudinous; what the eye lost in detail it gained in fullness. But in front stood a naked girl untouched by the reflections, her

weight on one leg, her hip thrust forward. Here Ingres' draftman-
ship was to be admired, but I actually found with satisfaction
that there was too much nakedness left in this girl even for the
sense of touch. From behind her came a gleam of pale, yellowish
light.

Dream 10. December 8, 1911, Age 28, Diaries 1, p. 172.

I then dreamed that I was in a very narrow but not very tall
glass-domed house with two entrances like the impassable pas-
sageways in the paintings of Italian primitives, also resembling
from the distance an arcade leading off from the Rue des Petits
Champs that we saw in Paris. Except that the one in Paris was
really wider and full of stores, but this one ran along between
blank walls, appeared to have scarcely enough room for two
people to walk side by side, but when one really entered it, as I
did with Mrs. Tschissik, there was a surprising amount of room,
which did not really surprise us. While I left by one exit with
Mrs. Tschissik in the direction of a possible observer of all this,
and Mrs. Tschissik at the same time apologized for some offense
or other (it seemed to be drunkenness) and begged me not to
believe her detractors, Mr. Tschissik, at the second of the house's
two exits, whipped a shaggy, blond St. Bernard which stood
opposite him on its hind legs. It was not quite clear whether he
was just playing with the dog and neglected his wife because of
it, or whether he had himself been attacked by the dog in
earnest, or whether he wished to keep the dog away from us.

(Mr. and Mrs. Tschissik were members of the Yiddish troupe
and Kafka was with them the day of this dream.)

Dream 11. May 6, 1912, Age 28, Diaries 1, pp. 260–61.

I was riding with my father through Berlin in a trolley. The
big-city quality was represented by countless striped toll bars
standing upright, finished off bluntly at the ends. Aside from that
everything was almost empty, but there was a great forest of
these toll bars. We came to a gate, got out without any sense of
getting out, stepped through the gate. On the other side of the
gate a sheer wall rose up, which my father ascended almost in a

dance, his legs flew out as he climbed, so easy was it for him. There was certainly also some inconsiderateness in the fact that he did not help me one bit, for I got to the top only with the utmost effort, on all fours, often sliding back again, as though the wall had become steeper under me. At the same time it was also distressing that (the wall) was covered with human excrement so that flakes of it clung to me, chiefly to my breast. I looked down at the flakes with bowed head and ran my hand over them.

When at last I reached the top, my father, who by this time was already coming out of a building, immediately fell on my neck and kissed and embraced me. He was wearing an old-fashioned, short Prince Albert, padded on the inside like a sofa, which I remembered well. "This Dr. von Leyden! He is an excellent man," he exclaimed over and over again. But he had by no means visited him in his capacity as doctor, but rather only as a man worth knowing. I was a little afraid that I should have to go in to see him too, but this wasn't required of me. Behind me to the left I saw, sitting in a room literally surrounded by glass walls, a man who turned his back on me. It turned out that this was the professor's secretary, that my father had in fact spoken only with him and not with the professor himself, but that somehow or other, through the secretary, he had recognized the excellences of the professor in the flesh, so that in every respect he was as much entitled to an opinion on the professor as if he had spoken to him in person.

(During this period Kafka was working on *Amerika*.)

Dream 12. July 10, 1912, Age 29, Diaries 2, *p. 304.*

I dreamt that I heard Goethe reciting with infinite freedom and arbitrariness.

(This dream occurred while Kafka was on a trip to Weimar. In Weimar, Kafka spent nearly all his time developing a relationship with the daughter of the caretaker of Goethe's house, who allowed him a freedom to explore the house and grounds not permitted the general public.)

Dream 13. July 15, 1912, Age 29, Diaries 2, p. 308.

The sunbathers destroyed one another in a brawl. After the two groups into which they were divided had joked with one another, someone stepped out in front of one group and shouted to the others: "Lustron and Kastron!" The others: "What? Lustron and Kastron?" He: "Right." Beginning of the brawl.

(After visiting Weimar, Kafka went to Jungborn which was a nature therapy establishment and nudist colony. This is where Kafka was called "the man in the swimming trunks.")

Dream 14. September 11, 1912, Age 29, Diaries 1, pp. 271–72.

I found myself on a jetty of square-cut stones built far out into the sea. Someone, or even several people, were with me, but my awareness of myself was so strong that I hardly knew more about them than I was speaking to them. I can remember only the raised knees of someone sitting near me. At first I did not really know where I was, only when once I accidentally stood up did I see on my left and behind me on my right the distant, clearly outlined sea with many battleships lined up in rows and at anchor. On the right New York could be seen, we were in New York Harbor. The sky was gray, but of a constant brightness. I moved back and forth in my seat, freely exposed to the air on all sides, in order to be able to see everything. In the direction of New York my glance slanted downward a little, in the direction of the sea it slanted upward. I now noticed the water rise up near us in high waves on which was borne a great cosmopolitan traffic. I can remember only that instead of the rafts we have, there were long timbers lashed together into gigantic bundles the cut ends of which kept popping out of the water during the voyage, higher or lower, according to the height of the waves, and at the same time kept turning end over end in the water. I sat down, drew up my feet, quivered with pleasure, virtually dug myself into the ground in delight, and said: Really, this is even more interesting than the traffic on a Paris boulevard.

(Kafka met Felice Bauer for the first time on August 20, 1912.

He was probably also working on *Amerika*. Kafka, of course, never visited the United States.)

Dream 15. July 21, 1913, Age 30, Diaries 1, *p. 291*.

Today, in my dream, I invented a new kind of vehicle for a park slope. You take a branch, it needn't be very strong, prop it up on the ground at a slight angle, hold one end in your hand, sit down on it sidesaddle, then the whole branch naturally rushes down the slope, since you are sitting on the bough you are carried along at full speed, rocking comfortably on the elastic wood. It is also possible to use the branch to ride up again. The chief advantage, aside from the simplicity of the whole device, lies in the fact that the branch, thin and flexible as it is, can be lowered or raised as necessary and gets through anywhere, even where a person by himself would get through only with difficulty.

("The Stoker" which was the first chapter of *Amerika* appeared in May, 1913.)

Dream 16. November 17, 1913, Age 30, Diaries 1, *pp. 307–8*.

On a rising way, beginning at the left when seen from below, there lay, about at the middle of the slope and mostly in the road, a pile of rubbish or solidly packed clay that had crumbled lower and lower on the right while on the left it stood up as tall as the palings of a fence. I walked on the right where the way was almost clear and saw a man on a tricycle coming toward me from below and apparently riding straight at the obstacle. He was a man who seemed to have no eyes, at least his eyes looked like holes that had been effaced. The tricycle was rickety and went along in an uncertain and shaky fashion, but nevertheless without a sound, with almost exaggerated quietness and ease. I seized the man at the last moment, held him as though he were the handle bars of his vehicle and guided the latter into the gap through which I had come. Then he fell toward me, I was as large as a giant now and yet had an awkward hold on him, besides, the vehicle, as though out of control, began to move backward, even if slowly, and pulled me after it. We went past an open van on which a number of people were standing crowded together, all dressed in dark clothes, among them a boy scout wearing a light-gray hat with the brim turned up. I expected this boy, whom I had already recognized at some distance, to help me, but he turned away and squeezed himself in among the people. Then, behind this open van—the tricycle kept rolling on and I, bent low with legs astraddle, had to follow—there came toward me someone who brought me help, but whom I cannot remember. I only know that he was a trustworthy person who is now concealing himself as though behind a black cloth curtain and whose concealment I should respect.

(Dreams 16–18. In September, 1913, Kafka stayed at a sanatorium in Riva. During this time he was working on "Metamorphosis." Troubles between Kafka and Felice Bauer began to appear.)

Dream 17. November 21, 1913, Age 30, Diaries 1, p. 310.

The French cabinet, four men, is sitting around a table. A conference is taking place. I remember the man sitting on the long right side of the table, with his face flattened out in profile, yellowish colored skin, his very straight nose jutting far forward (jutting so far forward because of the flatness of his face) and an oily, black, heavy mustache arching over his mouth.

Dream 18. November 24, 1913, Age 30, Diaries 1, pp. 311–12.

I am sitting in the garden of a sanatorium at a long table, at the very head, and in the dream I actually see my back. It is a gloomy day, I must have gone on a trip and am in an automobile that arrived a short time ago, driving up in a curve to the front of the platform. They are just about to bring in the food when I see one of the waitresses, a young, delicate girl wearing a dress the color of autumn leaves, approaching with a very light or unsteady step through the pillared hall that served as the porch of the sanatorium, and going down into the garden. I don't yet know what she wants but nevertheless point questioningly at myself to learn whether she wants me. And in fact she brings me a letter. I think, this can't be the letter I'm expecting, it is a very thin letter and a strange, thin, unsure handwriting. But I open it and a great number of thin sheets covered with writing come out, all of them in the strange handwriting. I begin to read, leaf through the pages and recognize that it must be a very important letter and apparently from F.'s youngest sister. I eagerly begin to read, then my neighbor on the right, I don't know whether man or woman, probably a child, looks down over my arm at the letter. I scream, "No!" The round table of nervous people begins to tremble. I have probably caused a disaster. I attempt to apologize with a few hasty words in order to be able to go on with the reading. I bend over my letter again, only to wake up without resistance, as if awakened by my own scream. With complete awareness I force myself to fall asleep again, the scene reappears, in fact I quickly read two or three more misty lines of the letter, nothing of which I can remember, and lose the dream in further sleep.

Dream 19. February 13, 1914, Age 30, Diaries 2, p. 19.

In Berlin, through the streets to her house, calm and happy in the knowledge that, though I haven't arrived at her house yet, a slight possibility of doing so exists; I shall certainly arrive there. I see the streets, on a white house a sign, something like "The Splendors of the North" (saw it in the paper yesterday); in my dream "Berlin W" has been added to it. Ask the way of an affable, red-nosed old policeman who in this instance is stuffed into a sort of butler's livery. Am given excessively detailed directions, he even points out the railing of a small park in the distance which I must keep hold of for safety's sake when I go past. Then advice about the trolley, the subway, etc. I can't follow him any longer and ask in a fright, knowing full well that I am underestimating the distance: "That's about half an hour away?" But the old man answers, "I can make it in six minutes." What joy! Some man, a shadow, a companion, is always at my side, I don't know who it is. Really have no time to turn around, to turn sideways.

(Dreams 19 and 20. During this time Kafka and Felice Bauer were not getting along. The "her" in Dream 19 is Felice Bauer who lived in Berlin.)

Dream 20. February 13, 1914, Age 30, Diaries 2, p. 20.

Live in Berlin in some pension or other apparently filled with young Polish Jews; very small rooms. I spill a bottle of water. One of them is tapping incessantly on a small typewriter, barely turns his head when he is asked for something. Impossible to lay hands on a map of Berlin. In the hand of one of them I continually notice a book that looks like a map. But it always proves to be something entirely different, a list of the Berlin schools, tax statistics, or something of the sort. I don't want to believe it, but, smiling, they prove it to me beyond any doubt.

Dream 21. December 2, 1914, Age 31, Diaries 2, p. 99.

Dreamed tonight. With Kaiser Wilhelm. In the castle. The beautiful view. A room similar to that in that Tabakskollegium. Meeting with Matilde Serav. Unfortunately forgot everything.

(Kafka finished the first draft of "In the Penal Colony" and was working on *The Trial*. About this time Kafka realized he could never marry Felice Bauer and broke off an engagement which had been made in May, 1914.)

Dream 22. January 19, 1915, Age 31, Diaries 2, pp. 109–10.

I had agreed to go picnicking Sunday with two friends, but quite unexpectedly slept past the hour when we were to meet. My friends, who knew how punctual I ordinarily am, were surprised, came to the house where I lived, waited outside awhile, then came upstairs and knocked on my door. I was very startled, jumped out of bed and thought only of getting ready as soon as I could. When I emerged fully dressed from my room, my friends fell back in manifest alarm. "What's that behind your head?" they cried. Since my awakening I had felt something preventing me from bending back my head, and I now groped for it with my hand. My friends, who had grown somewhat calmer, had just shouted "Be careful, don't hurt yourself!" when my hand closed behind my head on the hilt of a sword. My friends came closer, examined me, led me back to the mirror in my room and stripped me to the waist. A large, ancient knight's sword with a cross-shaped handle was buried to the hilt in my back, but the blade had been driven with such incredible precision between my skin and flesh that it had caused no injury. Nor was there a wound at the spot on my neck where the sword had penetrated; my friends assured me that there was an opening large enough to admit the blade, but dry and showing no trace of blood. And when my friends now stood on chairs and slowly, inch by inch, drew out the sword, I did not bleed, and the opening on my neck closed until no mark was left save a scarcely discernible slit. "Here is your sword," laughed my friends, and gave it to me. I hefted it in my two hands; it was a splendid weapon, Crusaders might have used it.

[Who tolerates this gadding about of ancient knights in dreams, irresponsibly brandishing their swords, stabbing innocent sleepers who are saved from serious injury only because the weapons in all likelihood glance off living bodies, and also because there are faithful friends knocking at the door, prepared to come to their assistance?]

(Kafka finished "the Village Schoolmaster" and a chapter in *Amerika*.)

Dream 23. September 29, 1915, Age 32, Diaries 2, pp. 131.

Many dreams. A combination of Marschner the director and Pimisker the servant appeared. Firm red cheeks, waxed black beard, thick unruly hair.

(Kafka begins to see Felice Bauer again.)

Dream 24. April 19, 1916, Age 32, Diaries 2, pp. 146–47.

We were living on the Graben near the Cafe Continental. A regiment turned in from Herrengasse on its way to the railroad station. My father: "That's something to look at as long as one can"; he swings himself up on the sill (in Felix's brown bathrobe, the figure in the dream was a mixture of the two) and with outstretched arms sprawls outside on the broad, sharply sloping window ledge. I catch hold of him by the two little loops through which the cord of his bathrobe passes. Maliciously, he leans even farther out, I exert all my strength to hold him. I think how good it would be if I could fasten my feet by ropes to something solid so that my father could not pull me out. But to do that I should have to let go of my father, at least for a short time, and that's impossible. Sleep,—my sleep, especially—cannot withstand all this tension and I wake up.

(Dreams 24–26. Kafka was sick during this time and was forced to take a leave from his position for medical treatment. In July, 1916, Kafka was living in Marienbad with Felice Bauer.)

Dream 25. April 20, 1916, Age 32, Diaries 2, pp. 147–48.

Two groups of men were fighting each other. The group to which I belonged had captured one of our opponents, a gigantic naked man. Five of us clung to him, one by the head, two on either side by his arms and legs. Unfortunately we had no knife with which to stab him, we hurriedly asked each other for a knife, no one had one. But since for some reason there was no time to lose and an oven stood nearby whose extraordinarily large cast-iron door was red-hot, we dragged the man to it, held one of his feet close to the oven until the foot began to smoke, pulled it back again until it stopped smoking, then thrust it close to the door again. We monotonously kept this up until I awoke, not only in a cold sweat but with my teeth actually chattering.

Dream 26. July 6, 1916, Age 33, Diaries 2, p. 158.

Dreamed of Dr. H.—he sat behind his desk, somehow leaning back and bending forward at the same time; limpid eyes; slowly and precisely, as is his way, pursuing an orderly train of thought to its end; even in the dream hear almost nothing of his words, simply follow the logic by which it is carried on. Then found myself beside his wife, who was carrying a lot of luggage and (what was astonishing) playing with my fingers; a patch was torn out of the thick felt of her sleeve, her arms took up only a small part of the sleeve, which was filled with strawberries.

Dream 27. September 19, 1917, Age 34, Diaries 2, p. 184.

Dreamed of Werfel: He was saying that in Lower Austria, where he is stopping at present, by accident he lightly jostled against a man on the street, whereupon the latter swore at him shamefully. I have forgotten the precise words, I remember only that one of them was "barbarian" (from the World War), and that it ended with "you proletarian Turch." An interesting combination: "Turch" is a dialect word for "Turk"; "Turk" is a curse word apparently still part of a tradition deriving from the old wars against the Turks and the sieges of Vienna, and added to that the new epithet, "proletarian." Excellently characterizes the simplicity and backwardness of his insulter, for today neither "proletarian" nor "Turk" is a real curse word.

(Dreams 27–29. In July, 1917, Kafka and Felice Bauer became engaged again. Kafka began coughing blood in August, 1917. On September 4, the disease was diagnosed as tuberculosis, and, on September 12, Kafka took convalescent leave to stay with his sister, Ottla, in the country. In December, he broke his second engagement with Felice Bauer.)

Dream 28. September 21, 1917, Age 34, Diaries 2, pp. 185–86.

A dream about my father: There was a small audience (to characterize it, Mrs. Fanta was there) before which my father was making public for the first time a scheme of his for social reform. He was anxious to have this select audience, an especially select one in his opinion, undertake to make propaganda for his scheme. On the surface he expressed this much more modestly, merely requesting the audience, after they should have heard his views to let him have the address of interested people who might be invited to a large public meeting soon to take place. My father had never yet had any dealings with these people, consequently took them much too seriously, had even put on a black frock coat, and described his scheme with that extreme solicitude which is the mark of an amateur. The company, in spite of the fact that they weren't at all prepared for a lecture, recognized at once that he was offering them, with all the pride of originality, what was

nothing more than an old, outworn idea that had been thorough-
ly debated long ago. They let my father feel this. He had antici-
pated the objection, however, and, with magnificent conviction of
its futility (though it often appeared to tempt even him), with
a faint, bitter smile, put his case even more emphatically. When
he had finished, one could perceive from the general murmur of
annoyance that he had convinced them neither of the originality
nor the practicability of his scheme. Not many were interested in
it. Still, here and there someone was to be found who, out of
kindness, and perhaps because he knew me, offered him a few
addresses. My father, completely unruffled by the general mood,
had cleared away his lecture notes and picked up the piles of
white slips that he had ready for writing down the few addresses.
I could hear only the name of a certain Privy Councillor Striza-
nowski, or something similar.

Later I saw my father sitting on the floor, his back against the
sofa, as he sits when he plays with Felix. Alarmed, I asked him
what he was doing. He was pondering his scheme.

Dream 29. November 10, 1917, Age 34, Diaries 2, pp. 190–91.

Dreamed of the battle of the Tagliamento. A plain, the river
wasn't really there, a crowd of excited onlookers ready to run
forward or backwards as the situation changed. In front of us a
plateau whose plainly visible edge was alternately bare and over-
grown with tall bushes. Upon the plateau and beyond Austrians
were fighting. Everyone was tense; what would be the outcome.
By way of diversion you could from time to time look at isolated
clumps on the dark slope, from behind which one or two Italians
were firing. But that had no importance, though we did take a
few steps backward in flight. Then the plateau again: Austrians
ran along the bare edge, pulled up abruptly behind the bushes,
ran again. Things were apparently going badly, and moreover it
was incomprehensible how they could ever go well; how could
one merely human being ever conquer other human beings who
were imbued with a will to defend themselves? Great despair,
there will have to be a general retreat. A Prussian major appeared

who had been watching the battle with us all the while; but when he calmly stepped forward into the suddenly deserted terrain, he seemed a new apparition. He put two fingers of each hand into his mouth and whistled the way one whistles to a dog, though affectionately. This was a signal to his detachment, which had been waiting close by and now marched forward. They were Prussian Guards, silent young men, not many, perhaps only a company, all seemed to be officers, at least they carried long sabers and their uniforms were dark. Then they marched by us, with short steps, slowly, in close order, now and then looking at us, the matter-of-factness of their death march was at once stirring, solemn and a promise of victory. With a feeling of relief at the intercession of these men, I woke up.

Dream 30. October 20, 1921, Age 38, Diaries 2, pp. 196–97.

A short dream, during an agitated, short sleep, in agitation clung to it with a feeling of boundless happiness. A dream with many ramifications, full of a thousand connections that become clear in a flash; but hardly more than a basic mood remains: My brother had committed a crime, a murder, I think, I and other people were involved in the crime; punishment, solution and salvation approached from afar, loomed up powerfully, many signs indicated their ineluctable approach; my sister, I think, kept calling out these signs as they appeared and I kept greeting them with insane exclamations, brief sentences merely, because of their succinctness, and now don't clearly remember a single one. I could only have uttered brief exclamations because of the great effort it cost me to speak—I had to puff out my cheeks and at the same time contort my mouth as if I had a toothache before I could bring a word out. My feeling of happiness lay in the fact that I welcomed so freely, with such conviction and such joy, the punishment that came, a sight that must have moved the gods, and I felt the god's emotion almost to the point of tears.

(Kafka met both Janouch and Milena Jesenská in early 1920, and these two people, especially Milena, were great influences on him during the following years. In 1921, Kafka stayed at a Tatra sanatorium.)

Dream 31. March 23, 1922, Age 38, Diaries 2, p. 225.

In the afternoon dreamed of a boil on my cheek. The perpetually shifting frontier that lies between ordinary life and the terror that would seem to be more real.

(Kafka was working on *The Castle*. In February, 1922, he returned to Prague from another health resort.)

Dream 32. 1920–23, Age 37–40, Letters to Milena, p. 43.

Recently I dreamed about you again, it was a long dream, but I remember hardly anything of it. I was in Vienna, of which I remember nothing, but then I came to Prague and had forgotten your address, not only the street but the town too, everything, only the name Schreiber came somehow to the surface but I didn't know what to do with it. So you were completely lost to me. In my despair I made several very cunning attempts which, however, I don't know why, were not carried through and of which I remember only one. I wrote on an envelope: Milena, and under it, "I beg that this letter be delivered, otherwise the Ministry of Finance will suffer an enormous loss." By this threat I hoped to set in motion all resources of the Government for your discovery.

(Dreams 32–37. During this period Kafka had a love affair with Milena Jesenská, a Czech writer, who was contributing articles to a Vienna newspaper at the time. Milena was married and contemplated divorcing her husband, but decided against it. Aside from "sick visits" to sanatoriums by Milena, the two met only twice, four days in Vienna and once more in Gmund when a rift began between them which widened until they finally broke off their relationship. Theirs was a "letter romance.")

Dream 33. 1920–23, Age 37–40, Letters to Milena, pp. 61–64.

. . . it was a proper city, toward evening, wet, dark, a vague sense of great traffic: the house in which I lived was separated from yours by a long, quadrangular public garden.

I had suddenly arrived in Vienna, had arrived ahead of my own letters which were still on the way to you (which later particularly grieved me). Nevertheless, you were informed and I was supposed to meet you. Luckily (though at the same time I also resented it) I was not alone, a small party, also a girl, I believe, were with me, but I don't know any details about them, they appeared to me somehow as my seconds. If only they would have kept quiet, but they talked incessantly, probably about my affairs, I heard only a nervous-making murmur, but understood nothing and didn't want to understand. I stood to the right of my house on the edge of the pavement and watched yours. It was a low villa with a beautiful simple stone loggia in front, reaching to the second floor.

Now it was suddenly breakfast time, the table was laid in the loggia, I saw from a distance how your husband arrived, sat down to the right in a cane chair, still drowsy and stretching himself with widespread arms. Then you came and sat down behind the table so that you could be fully seen. Not in detail though, it was so far away, the outlines of your husband could be seen much more distinctly, I don't know why, you remained just something blueish-whiteish, flowing, spectral. You also had your arms spread out, not however to stretch yourself, it was more of a ceremonious gesture.

Shortly afterwards, but now it was the precious evening, again, you were in the street with me, you were standing on the pavement, I with one foot on the road, I held your hand, and now a senseless, fast, short-sentenced conversation began, it went tit for tat and lasted almost uninterruptedly to the end of the dream.

I can't reproduce it, actually I remember only the two first and two last sentences, the middle part was one single torture impossible to convey.

Instead of a greeting I said quickly, persuaded by something in your face: "You imagined me to look different." You answered: "To be quite frank, I thought you would be more elegant" (actually, you used an even more Viennese expression, but I've forgotten it).

These were the first two sentences (in this connection it occurs to me: D'you realize that I'm completely unmusical, of a completeness which in my experience simply doesn't exist elsewhere?) and with them, in fact, everything was settled, what more could there be? But now began the argument about another meeting, the vaguest possible expressions on your part, incessant urgent questions on mine.

Now my companions interfered, an opinion was offered that I had also come to Vienna to visit an agricultural school in the neighborhood of Vienna, now it seemed after all as though I would have time to do this, obviously they were trying to get rid of me out of charity. Although I saw through this, I nevertheless went along to the station, no doubt hoping that such serious intentions to leave would make an impression on you. We all came to the station nearby, but now it turned out that I had forgotten the name of the place where the school was supposed to be. We stood in front of the large time-tables while someone kept running his finger down the names of the stations, asking me if it were perhaps this one or that, but it was none of them.

Meanwhile I had the chance to observe you a little, as a matter of fact it made no difference to me what you looked like, the only thing that mattered was your word. You didn't look much like yourself, in any case much darker, a thin face, no one with plump cheeks could have been so cruel. (But was it actually so cruel?) Your dress, strangely enough, was from the same material as my suit, was also very masculine, and I really didn't like it at all. But then I remembered a passage in a letter (the verse: . . .— "I only have two dresses, and still I look nice") and so great was the power of your word over me that from this moment I very much liked your dress.

But now the end had come, my companions were still searching the time-tables, we stood aside and argued. The last point of the argument was something like this: Next day was Sunday; to you it was incomprehensible to the point of repugnance how I could assume that you would have time for me on Sunday. Finally though, you apparently gave in and said you'd try and save 40 minutes for me. (The most awful part of this conversation was of course not the words, but the undertone, the uselessness of it all, as well as your continuous silent argument: "I don't want to come. So what good can it do you if I come all the same?") But just when you'd have these 40 minutes to spare I couldn't get out of you. You didn't know; in spite of all apparent concentrated thinking you couldn't decide. In the end I asked: "Shall I wait the whole day, perhaps?" "Yes," you said and turned away to a group of people who were standing there waiting for you. The meaning of the answer was that you wouldn't come at all and that the only concession you could make me was the permission to wait for you. "I won't wait," I said in a low voice, and as I thought you hadn't heard it and it was after all my last trump, I shouted it after you desperately. But it made no difference to you, you no longer paid any attention to it. Somehow I staggered back into town.

Dream 34. 1920–23, Age 37–40, Letters to Milena, *p. 67.*

Early this morning I dreamt about you again. We were sitting side-by-side and you were warding me off, not angrily, but friendly. I was very unhappy. Not about the warding off, but about myself who was treating you like any other silent woman and failed to hear the voice which spoke out of you and spoke expressly to me. Or perhaps it wasn't that I failed to hear it but that I couldn't have answered it. More hopelessly than in the first dream I walked away.

Dream 35. 1920–23, Age 37–40, Letters to Milena, *p. 130.*

Last night, I think for the first time since I'm in Prague, I dreamt of you. A dream toward morning, short and deep—I'd still caught some sleep after a bad night. I remember little about it. You were in Prague, we were walking down the Ferdinand-strasse, more or less opposite Vilimek in the direction of the Quay. Some acquaintances of yours walked past on the other side, we turned round after them, you spoke about them, perhaps there was also some talk about Krasa (he's not in Prague, this I know, I'll enquire about his address). You talked in a normal way but there was an intangible hidden element of rejection in it, I didn't mention it but cursed myself and in doing so only pronounced the curse that lay on me. Then we were in a coffee-house, probably the Cafe Union (it was on our road), at our table sat a man and a girl whom I can't remember at all, then a man who looked very much like Dostoevsky, but young with a dark black beard and hair—everything, the eyebrows for instance, the bone-structure above the eyes, very prominent. Then you and I were there. Again nothing betrayed your rejecting attitude, but the rejection was there. Your face was—I couldn't take my eyes off the tormenting peculiarity—powdered, and even exaggeratedly so, clumsy, bad, it was probably also hot and so whole designs of powder had formed on your cheeks, I can still see them before me. Again and again I leaned over to ask you why you were powdered; when you noticed that I was about to ask, you asked obligingly—as I say, the rejection couldn't be noticed—"What do you want?" But I couldn't ask, I didn't dare, and at the same time I guessed somehow that this being powdered was a test for me, a very decisive test—that I was meant to ask and even wanted to, but didn't dare. Thus the sad dream rolled over me. At the same time the Dostoevsky-man also tormented me. In his behavior towards me he was similar to you, but still somewhat different. When I asked him something he was very kind, co-operative, leaned over, frank, but when I couldn't think of anything more to ask or to say—which happened every moment—he drew back with a jerk, plunged into a book, took no more notice of the world, least of all of me, disappeared in his beard and hair. I don't know why this was unbearable to me, again and again I couldn't help it—I had to pull him over toward me with a question and again and again I lost him through my own fault.

Dream 36. 1920–23, Age 40, Letters to Milena, p. 159.

Someone, a relative, said in the course of a conversation which I don't remember but which had more or less the meaning that this or that person couldn't accomplish something—thus this relative said ironically at last: "Well, then perhaps Milena." Whereupon I killed him somehow, came home in great excitement, my mother running after me all the time, here too a similar conversation was taking place; at last hot with rage I cried out: "If anyone says anything bad about Milena, for instance the father (my father), I'll kill him too or myself."

Dream 37. 1920–23, Age 37–40, Letters to Milena, *p. 207*.

Last night I dreamt about you. What happened in detail I can hardly remember, all I know is that we kept merging into one another, I was you, you were me. Finally you somehow caught fire. Remembering that one extinguishes fire with clothing, I took an old coat and beat you with it. But again the transmutations began and it went so far that you were no longer even there, instead it was I who was on fire and it was also I who beat the fire with the coat. But the beating didn't help and it only confirmed my old fear that such things can't extinguish a fire. In the meantime, however, the fire brigade arrived and somehow you were saved. But you were different from before, spectral, as though drawn with chalk against the dark, and you fell, lifeless or perhaps having fainted from joy at having been saved, into my arms. But here too the uncertainty of transmutability entered, perhaps it was I who fell into someone's arms.

REFERENCES

ALLPORT, GORDON W. 1965. *Letters from Jenny*. New York: Harcourt, Brace & World.

ANONYMOUS. 1966. *Franz Kafka, 1883–1924*. Ausstellung der Akademie der Kunste.

BOLGAR, HEDDA. 1954. "Consistency of Affect and Symbolic Expression: A Comparison between Dreams and Rorschach Responses," *American Journal of Orthopsychiatry*, Vol. 24, pp. 538–45.

BONIME, WALTER. 1962. *The Clinical Use of Dreams*. New York: Basic Books.

BROD, MAX. 1963. *Franz Kafka: A Biography*. Translated from the German by G. H. Roberts (Chapters I to VII) and by R. Winston (Chapter VIII). New York: Schocken Books. (Abbreviation: B)

CATLIN, GEORGE E. G. 1965. "Library of Dreams," *International Journal of Social Psychiatry*, Vol. 11, No. 4, pp. 1–3.

COOK, W. ROLAND. 1956. "Nomothetic Personality Patterns in Dreams." Unpublished Ph.D. dissertation, Western Reserve University.

DODDS, E. R. 1965. *Pagan and Christian in an Age of Anxiety*. Cambridge, England: Cambridge University Press.

DOMHOFF, BILL, *and* JOE KAMIYA. 1964. "Problems in Dream Content Study with Objective Indicators: I. A Comparison of Home and Laboratory Dream Reports," *Archives of General Psychiatry*, Vol. 11, pp. 519–24.

EDEL, LEON. 1968. "Psychoanalysis and the 'Creative' Arts," in Judd Marmor (ed.). *Modern Psychoanalysis: New Directions and Perspectives*. New York: Basic Books.

FOULKES, DAVID, *and* ALLAN RECHTSCHAFFEN. 1964. "Presleep Determinants of Dream Content: Effects of Two Films," *Perceptual and Motor Skills Monograph Supplement*, Vol. 19, pp. 983–1005.

FRAIBERG, SELMA. 1963. "Kafka and the Dream," in William Phillips (ed.). *Art and Psychoanalysis*. Cleveland, Ohio: World Publishing Company.

FREUD, SIGMUND. 1918. "An Infantile Neurosis," in Vol. XVII, *Standard Edition of the Complete Psychological Works of Sigmund Freud*. London: Hogarth Press, 1955.

———. 1967. "Introduction," in Freud, Sigmund, and William C. Bullitt. *Thomas Woodrow Wilson*. Boston: Houghton Mifflin Company.

FROMM, ERICH. 1951. *The Forgotten Language*. New York: Grove Press.

GERBNER, GEORGE, et al. (eds.). 1969. *The Analysis of Communication Content*. New York: John Wiley & Sons, Inc.

GLASER, F. B. 1964. "The Case of Franz Kafka," *Psychoanalytic Review*, Vol. 51, pp. 99–121.

GOODMAN, PAUL. 1947. *Kafka's Prayer*. New York: Vanguard Press.

GORDON, HIRAM L. 1953. "A Comparative Study of Dreams and Responses to the Thematic Apperception Test: A Need-Press Analysis," *Journal of Personality*, Vol. 22, pp. 234–53.

GREEN, JULIAN. 1939. *Personal Record*. New York: Harper & Brothers.

GREENBERG, MARTIN. 1968. *The Terror of Art: Kafka and Modern Literature.* New York: Basic Books.

GROTZ, ROBERT C. 1950. "A Comparison of Thematic Apperception Test Stories and Manifest Dream Narratives." Unpublished Master's thesis, Western Reserve University.

HALL, CALVIN S. 1962. "Out of a Dream Came the Faucet," *Psychoanalysis and the Psychoanalytic Review*, Vol. 49, pp. 113–16.

———. 1964. "A Modest Confirmation of Freud's Theory of a Distinction between the Superego of Men and Women," *Journal of Abnormal and Social Psychology*, Vol. 69, pp. 440–42.

———. 1966a. *The Meaning of Dreams.* New York: McGraw-Hill.

———. 1966b. "A Comparison of the Dreams of Four Groups of Hospitalized Mental Patients with Each Other and with a Normal Population," *Journal of Nervous and Mental Disease*, Vol. 143, pp. 135–39.

———. 1969a. "Content Analysis of Dreams: Categories, Units, and Norms," in George Gerbner *et al.* (ed.). *The Analysis of Communication Content.* New York: John Wiley & Sons, Inc.

———. 1969b. "Normative Dream-Content Studies," in Milton Kramer (ed.). *Dream Psychology and the New Biology of Dreaming.* New York: Charles C. Thomas, Publisher.

———., and BILL DOMHOFF. 1963a. "A Ubiquitous Sex Difference in Dreams," *Journal of Abnormal and Social Psychology*, Vol. 66, pp. 278–80.

———. 1963b. "Aggression in Dreams," *International Journal of Social Psychiatry*, Vol. 9, pp. 259–67.

———. 1964. "Friendliness in Dreams," *Journal of Social Psychology.* Vol. 62, pp. 309–14.

———. 1968. "The Dreams of Freud and Jung," *Psychology Today*, Vol. 2, pp. 42–45, 64–65.

HALL, CALVIN S., *and* ROBERT L. VAN DE CASTLE. 1965. "An Empirical Investigation of the Castration Complex in Dreams." *Journal of Personality*, Vol. 33, pp. 20–29.

———. 1966a. *The Content Analysis of Dreams.* New York: Appleton-Century-Crofts.

———. 1966b. *Studies of Dreams Reported in the Laboratory and at Home.* ("Institute of Dream Research Monograph Series," No. 1.) Santa Cruz: Institute of Dream Research. 55 pp.

HELLER, ERIK. 1969. "The World of Franz Kafka," in Peter F. Neumeyer (ed.). *Twentieth Century Interpretations of The Castle.* Englewood Cliffs, New Jersey: Prentice-Hall.

HILL, BRIAN (ed.). 1968. *Gates of Horn and Ivory.* New York: Taplinger Publishing Co., Inc.

HOFFMAN, FREDERICK J. 1957. *Freudianism and the Literary Mind.* Baton Rouge, La.: Louisiana State University Press.

HORTON, LYDIARD H. 1925. *Dissertation on the Dream Problem*. 2 vols. Cartesian Research Society of Philadelphia.

HOWELLS, WILLIAM D. 1895. "True I Talk of Dreams." *Harper's Magazine*, Vol. 40, pp. 836–45.

HUBBEN, WILLIAM. 1962. *Dostoevsky, Kierkegaard, Nietzsche, and Kafka*. New York: Collier Books.

IONESCO, EUGÈNE. 1969. *Fragments of a Journal*. New York: Grove Press.

JAGER, BERND. 1968. "Three Dreams of Descartes: A Phenomenological Exploration." *Review of Existential Psychology and Psychiatry*, Vol. 8, pp. 195–213.

JANOUCH, GUSTAV. 1953. *Conversations with Kafka*. Translated by Goronwy Rees. London: Derek Verschoyle.

JUNG, CARL G. 1934. "The Practical Use of Dream-Analysis," in Vol. 16, *Collected Works of C. G. Jung*. New York: Pantheon Books, 1954.

KAFKA, FRANZ. 1937. *The Trial*. Translated by Willa and Edwin Muir. New York: Modern Library.

———. 1946. *Amerika*. Translated by Edwin Muir. New York: New Directions.

———. 1948. *The Penal Colony: Stories and Short Pieces*. Translated by Willa and Edwin Muir. New York: Schocken Books.

———. 1954. "The Eight Octavo Note-Books and Fragments from Notebooks and Loose Pages," in *Wedding Preparations in the Country and Other Posthumous Writings*. London: Secker and Warburg. (Abbreviation: Fragments)

———. 1957. *The Castle*. Translated by Willa and Edwin Muir. Harmondsworth, England: Penguin.

———. 1958. *Briefe, 1902–1924*. New York: Schocken Books.

———. 1962. *Letters to Milena*. Translated by Tania and James Stern. New York: Schocken Books. (Abbreviation: M)

———. 1965. *Diaries*, Vol. 1, 1910–13. Translated by Joseph Kresh. Vol. 2, 1914–23. Translated by Martin Greenberg with the co-operation of Hannah Arendt. New York: Schocken Books. (Abbreviations: D1 and D2)

———. 1966. *Letter to His Father*. Translated by Ernst Kaiser and Eithne Wilkins. New York: Schocken Books. (Abbreviation: LF)

———. 1969. *The Trial*. New York: Schocken Books.

KEROUAC, JACK. 1961. *Book of Dreams*. San Francisco: City Lights Books.

KINSEY, A. C., W. B. POMEROY, and C. E. MARTIN. 1948. *Sexual Behavior in the Human Male*. Philadelphia: W. B. Saunders Co.

LOWIE, ROBERT H. 1966. "Dreams, Idle Dreams," *Current Anthropology*, Vol. 7, pp. 378–82.

MCCURDY, HAROLD G. 1961. *The Personal World*. New York: Harcourt, Brace, and World.

———. 1965. *Personality and Science*. Princeton, New Jersey: D. Van Nostrand Co., Inc.

————. 1968. "The Anatomy of Dreams." Presidential address, Chapter of Sigma Xi, The University of North Carolina.

MANN, L. 1955. "The Relation of Rorschach Indices of Extraversion-Introversion to Certain Dream Dimensions," *Journal of Clinical Psychology*, Vol. 11, pp. 80–81.

MEER, SAMUEL J. 1955. "Authoritarian Attitudes and Dreams," *Journal of Abnormal and Social Psychology*, Vol. 51, pp. 74–78.

NEIDER, CHARLES. 1962. *The Frozen Sea: A Study of Franz Kafka*. New York: Russell and Russell.

NEMEROV, HOWARD. 1965. *Journal of the Fictive Life*. New Brunswick, New Jersey: Rutgers University Press.

OSGOOD, CHARLES E. 1959. "The Representation Model and Relevant Research Methods," in I. de Sola Pool (ed.). *Trends in Content Analysis*. Urbana, Illinois: University of Illinois Press.

POLITZER, HEINZ. 1962. *Franz Kafka: Parable and Paradox*. Ithaca, New York: Cornell University Press.

RYCHLAK, JOSEPH F. 1960. "Recalled Dream Themes and Personality," *Journal of Abnormal and Social Psychology*, Vol. 60. pp. 140–43.

————., *and* JEROME M. BRAMS. "Personality Dimensions in Recalled Dream Content," *Journal of Projective Techniques*, Vol. 27, pp. 226–34.

SARASON, SEYMOUR B. 1944. "Projective Techniques in Mental Deficiency," *Journal of Personality*, Vol. 13, pp. 237–45.

SCHORER, MARK. 1949. "Fiction and the 'Matrix of Analogy'," *Kenyon Review*, Vol. 11, pp. 539–60.

SEDELOW, SALLY Y., *and* WALTER A. SEDELOW, JR. 1966. "A Preface to Computational Stylistics," in Jacob Leed (ed.). *The Computer and Literary Style*. Kent, Ohio: Kent State University Press, pp. 1–13.

————. 1969. "Categories and Procedures for Content Analysis in the Humanities," in George Gerbner *et al.* (eds.) *The Analysis of Communication Content*. New York: John Wiley & Sons, Inc.

SEYPPEL, J. H. 1956. The Animal Theme and Totemism in Franz Kafka," *American Imago*, Vol. 13, pp. 69–93.

SHULMAN, HAROLD S. 1955. "Congruences of Personality Expression in Self-Conceptions, Thematic Apperception Test, and Dreams." Unpublished Ph.D. dissertation, Western Reserve University.

SMITH, MADORAH E., *and* CALVIN S. HALL. 1964. "An Investigation of Regression in a Long Dream Series," *Journal of Gerontology*, Vol. 19, pp. 66–71.

SOKEL, WALTER H. 1966. *Franz Kafka*. New York: Columbia University Press.

SPILKA, MARK. 1963. *Dickens and Kafka: A Mutual Interpretation*. Bloomington, Indiana: Indiana University Press.

SPURGEON, CAROLINE. 1935. *Shakespeare's Imagery and What It Tells Us*. New York: The Macmillan Co.

STONE, PHILIP J., et al. 1966. *The General Inquirer: A Computer Approach to Content Analysis.* Cambridge, Massachusetts: The M.I.T. Press.

URZIDIL, JOHANNES. 1968. *There Goes Kafka.* Translated by Harold A. Basilius. Detroit, Michigan: Wayne State University Press.

VAN DE CASTLE, ROBERT L. 1968. "A Contingency Analysis of Dreams Containing Animal Figures." Paper given at the annual meeting of the Association for the Psychophysiological Study of Sleep, Denver, Colorado.

WHITE, JOHN S. 1967. "Psyche and Tuberculosis: The Libido Organization of Franz Kafka." in Warner Muensterberger and Sidney Axelrad (eds.). *The Psychoanalytic Study of Society.* New York: International Universities Press.

WHITE, RALPH K. 1947. "*Black Boy*: A Value Analysis," *Journal of Abnormal and Social Psychology*, Vol. 42, pp. 440–61.

WINGET, CAROLYN. 1967. "Hostility in the Dreams of Negro and White Males." Unpublished Master's thesis, University of Cincinnati.

WISDOM, J. O. 1947. "Three Dreams of Descartes," *International Journal of Psychoanalysis*, Vol. 28, pp. 11–18.

INDEX

Text set in Linotype Electra
COMPOSITION, PRINTING BY
Heritage Printers, Inc., Charlotte, North Carolina
BINDING BY
Kingsport Press, Kingsport, Tennessee
Sixty-pound Olde Style paper by
S. D. Warren Company, Boston, Massachusetts
DESIGNED AND PUBLISHED BY
The University of North Carolina Press
Chapel Hill, North Carolina

DATE DUE